Advance praise for The Co-Cr

The Co-Creation Handbook *is a brilliant book which provides a step by step guide to access your creative potential. Alida Birch's writing is clear and personal. It feels like she is right by your side as you uncover your soul's desire and take steps to manifest it.*
—Sandra Ingerman, MA author of *Medicine for the Earth* and *The Shaman's Toolkit*

I highly recommend The Co-Creation Handbook! *I found it simple and easy to follow. I focused on manifesting clients for my distance healing work. Within a month, I had a full schedule. The Co-Creation work in alignment with the Universal Powers was what brought this abundance into my life.*
—Rita Baxter, LMT, soul response therapist & shamanic practitioner. Shamana Massage & Healing

I love this book! Alida Birch has provided the reader with a practical, applicable and clear process for accessing, mobilizing and directing the creative pulse within us. This pulse is a spark of the Divine Flame, our Essential Nature and God-Within and . . . its destiny is creativity. This book leads us to personal magic, conscious choice and joyous discipline through ancient shamanic wisdom and contemporary practice . . . a literary marriage destined to bear happiness.
—Orion Foxwood, author of *The Tree of Enchantment* and *The Candle and the Crossroads*

You only have to follow this clearly laid out process to call forth your dreams! Three years ago I began working with The Co-Creation Handbook. *On a small slip of paper I wrote down: "I want to manifest a rock and roll band." At the time I had a guitar and some songs and really not much more in the way of music. The synchronicities that followed were astounding and joyful! Now, three years later I am the lead singer, songwriter and guitar player in a touring rock and roll band called Blue Lotus. Magic happens . . . This course changed my life—literally. Love you Alida! Thank you!*
—Brandelyn Rose, Blue Lotus

The Co-Creation Handbook *is a clear and useful guide for all who wish to take a more active role in co-creating a healthier and happier reality for their daily lives. Drawing on recent consciousness studies and the ancient practices of shamanism, Alida Birch shows us how to envision and manifest a more soul-full and spiritually rewarding life.*
—Tom Cowan, PhD, author of *Fire in the Head: Shamanism and the Celtic Spirit*; and *Shamanism as a Spiritual Practice for Daily Life*

Within a month of completing The Co-Creation Handbook, *my life shifted. It became clear to me what my passion was and how to fulfill it. Within the first year I developed "A Course on Happiness" and created my new business, all due to learning how to manifest. Thank you!*
—Barb Ryan, M.S., *Guidess of Happiness*
SpiralingTowardJoy.org

Alida Birch has crafted a remarkable handbook of co-creation of our lives. With its accompanying audio program, this is a most helpful tool, where she gently and compassionately guides the reader, linking the shamanic practice to the manifestation process. With clarity and generosity she plunges in the depth of her own life experience to bring the handbook to life. The Co-Creation Handbook *leads the reader through exercises and practices to be the True Nature, Authentic Being that we are.* The Co-Creation Handbook *is a timely and welcome guide that beautifully invites us to collaborate within ourselves, with the Spirits, and with the Universe, so as to co-create a world that is in harmony with the Divine.*
—Claude Poncelet, PhD author of *The Shaman Within*

A few summers ago I was sequestered in a cabin in Michigan, with the opportunity to inescapably relive my childhood experiences, like reruns of Leave it to Beaver *gone wrong. My saving grace was* The Co-Creation Handbook *course. I vigilantly did the morning and evening audio sessions, and I took the long days to face my reality, accept it, and make my choices. It really made all the difference, and I can look back now at that time and call it a gift. This work is our ongoing life challenge. Every day we must step into our vision with full conviction, honor reality as it is, and feel that creative tension. When I don't, I languish. When I do, my whole being moves forward, and I am able to live my life to the fullest. I encourage you to choose to give your full attention to this program. It will serve you in every regard.*
—Carla Meeske, Shamanic Practitioner & Animal Communicator, author of *The Calico Shaman*, Spirithealer.com

Alida Birch's The Co-Creation Handbook *is a clear, loving and detailed eight-week program for supporting you to realize your inherent capacity as a Divine Co-Creator. Using the foundation of 100,000 years of shamanic wisdom with clear exercises and supportive audios you will learn how to clarify your vision, identify your stumbling blocks and persistently move forward with a sense of gratitude and happiness. Your magnificent life is waiting for you to participate in its creation. Start now.*
—Evelyn C. Rysdyk
Author of *Spirit Walking: A Course in Shamanic Power*

The Co-Creation Handbook

A Shamanic Guide to
Manifesting a Better World
and a More Joyful Life

ALIDA BIRCH

LUMINARE PRESS
EUGENE, OREGON

The Co-Creation Handbook
© 2014 Alida Birch
www.alidabirch.com
www.co-creationhandbook.com

Printed in the United States of America

Cover Illustration: Shelley Masters
Cover Photo credit: Peggy Iileen Johnson
Cover Design: Claire Last

Luminare Press
467 W 17th Ave
Eugene, OR 97401
www.luminarepress.com

ISBN: 978-1-937303-39-6

LCCN: 2014954269

Dedicated to the hummingbird
who shows me time and time again
how possible the improbable is.

Contents

Introduction

I AM STARTING out this book by telling you what it is not. I know this is unusual but it is essential for you to understand the difference between this and every other manifestation book out there. This is not another one of those "over-sensationalized, promise-you-everything-ra-ra-you-can-have-it-all" handbooks. Due to the proliferation of books written on manifesting, especially since *The Secret*, there is now a popular misperception that we can manifest anything we want – all we have to do is think about it, have the focused intention and it will be so. And, I might add, there are a lot of disappointed people out there wondering why this didn't work for them. It is obvious to me that there are huge pieces of the puzzle missing and it is these critical pieces I will help you to master.

What we do know is that humans are powerful manifestors, but our times demand much more from us than simply creating what we want. Our planet is in deep trouble and we are responsible. We have created so much in such a short time because our vision has been short sighted and egocentric, resulting in the loss of precious resources and entire species. Now we are faced with the possibility that our planet may not be sustainable for future generations. It is time to harness our creativity to a greater purpose and join hands with wise and powerful allies that can help guide our efforts.

What is this handbook all about? Quite simply it is about stepping into your role as a Co-Creator of this magnificent universe we live in by learning how to be a partner in creating. The partnership is with the subtle beings of the many planes of existence. I think of them as Helping Spirits, Divine Beings, Spirit Teachers and the Universal Powers. You may know of them as fairies, Devas, the Shining Ones, or Angels. There are many names for these spiritual beings and I am sure you even may know some I don't.

These loving and compassionate beings of the Spirit World are waiting for you to request their help and will be here to walk with you through the many experiences you will encounter along the way. Given willingness on your part, a willingness to truly transform, you will find that during the next eight weeks the Spirit World will open up to you. The Spirit Helpers you will

[handwritten margin note: Co-create with subtle beings of many planes of existence]

meet have a special interest in helping you to develop your gifts and nurture your ability to manifest. They, too, have an agenda. They wish to serve the planet as a whole and all life upon it. This Co-Creative partnership will help you to use your creative gifts to expand your vision to manifest a better world and a more joyful life.

The first part of this book is all about igniting and nurturing your ability to co-create. You will learn the technology of creating, those essential lessons for navigating skillfully through life. You will practice by creating small goals that will serve to help you learn the structure of creating. Then you will learn how to safely accelerate the creative process by partnering with the Divine Beings of the Spirit World using a method shamans have used for over 100,000 years: the shamanic journey.

The shamanic journey is the most ancient spiritual practice known to humankind. It is a safe, practical method for discovering hidden spiritual resources and transforming lives.

You will find the shamanic journey is a simple and unique way to restore and expand your creative powers. The shamanic journey is a reliable method for accessing a non-ordinary state of consciousness—an important skill for becoming a Co-Creator. This non-ordinary reality will open you up to an extraordinary range of guidance, healing and assistance, enhancing and accelerating your Co-Creative Process. Through the Audio Program, you will learn to journey to your Spirit Helpers and Spirit Teachers, and through them you will learn how to gain critical information, access ancient wisdom, expand your perspective, and also receive assistance should you encounter personal blocks to manifestation.

> Here when I speak of power I am referring to *power with* not *power over*. This is not the power of the self-aggrandized ego. It is power to be used to nurture our world for the benefit of all beings. The shamanic worldview invites you to the great web of life and teaches us that we are all connected.

The Audio Program is an absolutely essential component of this process, creating within you a container for this work to take hold. Twice daily, beginning with Week One, the Audio Program leads you through a spiritual odyssey that will hugely expand your ability to co-create yet requires only 20 minutes of your day. When you use the Audio Program consistently, your progress is accelerated exponentially.

The Audio Program is available for download at:
www.Co-CreationHandbook.com.
The password is: hummingbird

Eight weeks to making a major shift in your life

YOU WILL BENEFIT the most by working the handbook through all eight weeks in sequence from start to finish. You will find each week introduces key concepts that will build on the previous weeks' work. Going from start to finish will give you a strong foundation for understanding the Co-Creative Process and fully integrating the concepts into your way of being in the world.

There is another reason I have designed this course to be eight weeks in length: the latest research in neuroscience indicates that we require at least eight weeks of consistent effort to make a behavioral shift permanent and form new neural pathways in our brain.[1] Eight weeks is the minimum. If you are serious about claiming your birthright as a Co-Creator, then you will continue to work with these universal principles in a disciplined way in the weeks, months and years to come. If you choose to do so, you will be well on your way to becoming the Predominant Creative Force[2] in your life by consciously creating those things that *truly* matter to you.

For those concerned about aging and its detrimental effects on the brain, there is no better elixir of youth than staying mentally sharp by continually creating that which is most truly important to you. In these eight weeks, you will be learning key new concepts which will enable you to restructure your understanding of the Co-Creative Process and greatly strengthen your ability to create, regardless of how young or old you are.

So, are you ready? Then let's begin!

Four Principles to Get You Started

BEFORE WE GET down to the nuts and bolts of co-creating, let's cover four essential concepts, which—once understood and applied—will change how you think, feel, and act. Most importantly, they will change how effective you are at co-creating.

Principle #1: Happiness is a Fundamental Choice.

> *Each morning when I open my eyes I say to myself: I, not events, have the power to make me happy or unhappy today. I can choose which it shall be. Yesterday is dead, tomorrow hasn't arrived yet. I have just one day, today, and I'm going to be happy in it.*
>
> —Groucho Marx

IF SOMETHING BRINGS us or others happiness, we want to create it, do it, or be in relationship with it. Everyone wants to manifest happiness. But until recently, few understood how essential happiness is to all we are attempting to accomplish.

Research is revealing that there are three key influences to your happiness level: set point, circumstances, and intentional activity. The set point is what you were born with, genetics. Circumstance is the situation you find yourself in. The intentional activity is your coping strategy, your behavior. Set point accounts for fifty percent of our happiness level, circumstance accounts for ten percent and intentional activity accounts for forty percent.[3]

If you are discouraged after reading this bit of information because your set point is stuck in unhappiness, let me share with you my story. My mother was an unhappy woman and, as mothers usually are a role model for their daughters, my mother was my role model. I learned from her to be unhappy. Because of this upbringing, I did not understand that happiness was something I could choose.

In my early years, I often felt victimized and blamed others for my unhappiness, just as my mother did. I was so caught up in this cycle of unhappiness that I often felt hopeless and, sometimes as a teenager, I contemplated suicide. Any challenging situation could send me reeling into an unhappy state because I was dependent on outside circumstances to feel happy. As a result, my set point for happiness was dangerously close to zero.

Over the years, I watched others respond to situations which would have devastated me and I marveled at their resiliency. They were always optimistic yet grounded in their everyday reality and that was much different from how I was experiencing my life. I made a choice to build up my resiliency and nurture my natural optimism. Finally, when the research on happiness I have just shared with you came out, I understood all I had perceived.

Now that I had a framework to put it in, I realized I still had that other fifty percent (circumstance plus intentional activity) to work with and I formally made the fundamental choice to be happy. For me, it was a watershed moment. Then I was stubborn about my choice to be happy —no one was going to take it away from me. Happiness did not descend on me all at once. It took awhile, but my happiness level is quite a bit higher than before.

I had a great deal to learn about choosing happiness. It is a journey and I invite you to take a step towards it each day. This first week the Audio Program will focus on helping you to choose happiness.

Now we come to the big questions:

Why is happiness helpful in the Co-Creative Process?

Does a state of happiness enable us to create faster?

I found the answer to these questions in an ancient text called The Emerald Tablet which states:

As below, so above; and as above, so below.
With this knowledge alone you may work miracles.[4]

Said in another way, what you hold in your mind (below) is a reflection of the Divine (above); what you hold in your mind causes a shift in the reflection of the Divine as well. Therefore, you are a creator. The Divine is the primary and original Creator. So we adopt for ourselves the title of Co-Creator. (You did want a title, right?)

This does not mean that Co-Creators are on a level with the Divine. This means that whether you are aware of it or not, you are always in a collaborative adventure with the great Universal Powers. Really, the key is to simply become aware of it. Then, once you become aware of it, *learn how to make use of it.*

You may also have heard the phrase, "As within, so without." When you send out your intention, you impact your entire world. Therefore, you are manifesting a world that sends back to you whatever it is that you send out. This world takes whatever energy you radiate and reflects it back to you just as a mirror reflects your image back to you. What this means is this: if you express anger, you will get anger reflected back. If you express creative, fulfilling, uplifting energy, it will come right back to you. Sometimes there is a time delay and sometimes the reflection is subtle, but it is there. This is how thoughts become things.[5]

A further step, as we acknowledge "as above, so below, as within, so without," is the realization that we are indeed all ONE. The spiritual and the physical are not two worlds, but ONE world. When we engage in this Co-Creative Process, we are experiencing the wholeness of a living vital system.

And now, consider this: since we want to manifest what makes us and others happy and following the premise that thoughts become things, we want to make the obvious choice to choose happiness. While this sounds simple enough, I know for many of you it is not. For me, choosing happiness was one of the most challenging practices of my inner environment. I had to learn to constantly monitor and redirect my innermost thoughts.

The good news is that the hardest part is in the beginning, and it does get easier with practice. It will for you, too, especially because you will have eight weeks of support via this handbook and the Audio Program.

What I say to you now is this: no matter what you are experiencing in your outer environment, *you can choose an inner environment of happiness*. You do not have to let what is going on outside you control what is going on inside you. As Shawn Achor, a leading expert on the connection between happiness and success, reminds us, "ninety percent of our long term happiness is predicted by the way our brain processes the world, not by external circumstances. If we change our formula for happiness and success, what we can do is change the way that we can then affect reality."[6]

The following example is simple, but really brought home to me the concept that happiness is an inside job. I remember so clearly seeing a comparison of people that were happy with their shoes: The first person was a wealthy western woman with an obviously expensive pair of brand new stilettos. The second person was an inner city teenager with a worn out pair of Nikes. The third person was from a third world country, dressed in rags, with just a strip of cardboard tied to his feet with rope. All were grinning broadly as they referred to their shoes. It was not the shoe but their perspective of the shoe that made them happy. These people were happy because they perceived that they had wonderful shoes.

You can be happy right now. It is a fundamental choice. And when you make the fundamental choice to be happy, it is much easier to move toward all those goals and visions you have. The happiness that lights you up on the inside will be reflected back to you in everyone you meet and everything you do.

You may be surprised to think of happiness as a fundamental choice. Most of us are taught that happiness is identified as a feeling state, when in fact it is more helpful to think of happiness as a *choice*. When we shift our thinking to "happiness is a *choice*" then we are in a position of power.

We can and do choose happiness.

> The Co-Creative journey is not about "finding happiness." Choose happiness now at the start of your journey. Then make the journey about creating those things that are most dear to you from a place of happiness.

Postponing Happiness

Common reasons for waiting for happiness are:

- ✧ If only I was rich, then I'd be happy.[7]
- ✧ If only I was famous, then I'd be happy.
- ✧ If only I could find the right person to marry, then I'd be happy.
- ✧ If only I was more attractive, then I'd be happy.
- ✧ If only I wasn't physically handicapped in any way, then I'd be happy.
- ✧ If only someone close to me hadn't died, then I'd be happy.
- ✧ If only the world was a better place, then I'd be happy.[8]
- ✧ If only I had a better childhood, then I'd be happy.

All of these statements fall into the category of waiting for something beyond your control to change either through a change in circumstance or a change in someone else's behavior. To wait for something to change before you allow yourself to be happy makes no sense.

> To wait for happiness to happen is a thinking error.

Happiness comes from the heart. Because it is an internal experience, nothing external can create happiness. *Nothing.*

As we come to an understanding of how to choose happiness, we realize that there is no reason to postpone it. And yet we all do, because most of us were taught as children to believe happiness had to be earned—that we had to do something, fix something, accomplish something, please someone, or make someone else feel happy before we could feel happy. We were taught that happiness is conditional. We were taught that if anyone around us is suffering, we have no right to feel happiness.

Most of us are trained from an early age to focus on what is *not* working and to feel bad or guilty about those not working things because *we* must be at fault—or something similar to this. So choosing happiness is, for most of us, a radical departure from the norm.

Do not wait until happiness descends upon you and do not tie your happiness to events or people you have no control over.

Here is an example of how someone delays his happiness:

Earl is not happy until he completely finishes his work assignment. He denies himself the happiness of actually doing the job itself. Once the assignment is done, he begins to look for his next assignment because he believes he must always be working. So he never gives himself the time to be happy with a job well done. As a result, his time for happiness is the tiny sliver of space between finishing one assignment and beginning another.

The truth is we can experience happiness, right now—anytime, anywhere, and in any circumstance. All you have to do is choose happiness. If you find some resistance to this concept, then it would be an excellent idea to take a closer look at what you were taught as a child about when you are allowed to be happy. Then decide if those beliefs are still serving you. Is it time to exchange those old beliefs for ones that help you rather than hinder you? Is it time to claim happiness in this moment?

Identifying how we deny ourselves happiness in the present moment is a vital step in our healing process. We must take the time to heal those parts of ourselves that are blocking our creativity or we will find it very difficult to bring our dreams into reality.

EXERCISE: HOW YOU DELAY HAPPINESS

How are you delaying happiness? Can you think of 3-5 ways you postpone happiness? What were you taught as a small child about how to be happy?

_____

_____

_____

_____

_____

In this Co-Creative Process, our first step is to make the fundamental choice to be happy.

You may find thoughts such as these running through your mind: "How can I be happy when children are starving, there are homeless people, my dog is sick, or my sister got fired?"

> Consider this: you are the only life you are in charge of, therefore you are the only person you can make happy. Choosing happiness is basic self care. If you don't choose it for you, no one else can.
> Happiness is a fundamental choice and key to everything we are about to do in manifesting all that is important to you in your life.

If you find you are having difficulty in choosing happiness for yourself, you may believe that you are being selfish because you want to be happy when those around you are not. Here is one way to shift your attitude about this kind of thinking. If you model happiness, then others (your children, your friends, and your co-workers) will be affected by the happiness vibration you exude. Your happiness will be reflected back to you. Those around you will feel uplifted. Perhaps you can remember a time when you were in the presence of someone who was consistently happy with life, no matter what was given them. They light up a room just by walking into it. In that same way, you can influence others around you toward happiness. Invite them to choose happiness by first choosing happiness for yourself.

Are you ready to learn how? (Drum roll please!):

How to choose happiness…There is no mystery here. You just choose it. It is a decision. You simply decide you are going to be happy no matter what else happens around you. You make it a fundamental choice in your life.

Here is one specific exercise you can do to choose happiness: When you wake up each morning - before you get out of bed - consciously decide "I choose happiness today." Notice I didn't say, "I am *going* to be happy…" I said, "I *choose happiness* today." Say "I choose happiness" out loud three times. You may also spend two minutes thinking of all the ways you are happy. For now, bring into your consciousness all the moments in your life when you have experienced happiness. Think about all the things you are already doing to bring even more happiness into your life. Reflect on all the beauty in your life, in nature, and in the world all around you. See how many different ways you can enjoy finding even more happiness in your life. Right here. Right now.

There, that is one of the big secrets. Pay attention to this. Choosing happiness in this moment will change your life. Notice I never asked you to "be happy." I am asking you to "make the fundamental choice to be happy." Can you sense the energetic difference between these two phrases?

One tells you to be a certain way.

The other asks you to become the Predominant Creative Force in your life by choosing.

Choosing is powerful.

You may find it takes a large effort on your part to choose happiness. Could this be because of an old habit you may have - the habit of choosing not to be happy? You've already been making a choice, just the wrong one! Perhaps making this choice has become effortless, when you stop to think about it, because it is a habit. You choose your happiness level all the time whether you think about it or not. Happiness is a habit. Habits can be changed because the brain can change.

There used to be a belief that we could not change the structure of our brains as we got older, but this is not true. It has now been proven even the elderly can rewire neural pathways through proper stimulation. And if the elderly can rewire their neural pathways, then everyone can, including you.

This concept is called neuroplasticity and points to the ability of the brain to continue growing and reorganizing itself as a result of stimulation, regardless of age, IQ, or physical limitations. It means that you can change your brain by creating new habits.

One of the habits you can change is the choice you are consistently making about your happiness level. You may not have the perfect life or partner or job or bank account, but as you may already have figured out, those things do not bring happiness to your life.

You bring happiness *all by itself* to you and it is a conscious and fundamental choice in your life.

Your choice.

Another way to choose happiness is by choosing to be grateful. It's been proven: those who practice the art of gratefulness are much happier.[9] I call it an art because by focusing on gratitude you are reprogramming your brain to be in a state of awe and wonder at the magic of your life and all that surrounds you.

> Gratitude brings you powerfully into the present moment of now.
> Happiness is a lovely by-product of gratitude.

So what is gratitude? It is savoring and relishing what you have in the present moment. It can be as simple as looking on the positive side of an experience, acknowledging what is going well in your life, thanking the relationships you have in your life, or thanking God or what you perceive as the Divine.

When I focus on what I am grateful for, I go directly to Source. I contemplate that by luck, Divine intervention, or perhaps my soul's conscious choice, I am here on this planet. Out of all the billions of possibilities of what could have combined to produce me, I am exactly who I am now with the consciousness that resides in my soul. I am so grateful I get to experience this life, the people I relate too, and this beautiful earth that surrounds and nourishes me.

You may want to keep a gratefulness journal. Write daily of just a few of the things you are grateful for. Keep it handy so if you are having trouble remembering why you are grateful, it's all right there in front of you. You just have to remember to read it.

Principle #2
Being in the Flow of Manifestation Brings You Joy

Only in joy does creation take place.
—Rilke

JOY IS A deep sense of alignment with your purpose. It is an inner knowing that what you are doing is right for you. For many of us, joy feels like a spiritual experience, a type of sacred barometer. Some people describe joy as an inner knowing, a sense that they have come home.

Happiness is a fundamental choice. Joy is a result of living out your fundamental choice to be happy and being in the flow of your purpose, your destiny.

When you clearly define and move towards your purpose while making the fundamental choice to be happy, you will notice that a flow begins to happen inside you. I personally feel this flow as a warm glow residing somewhere between my solar plexus and heart, sometimes as a gently insistent pressure nudging me forward. You may feel it in an entirely different way. If you allow yourself to relax into the flow and move with it, joy will arise.

Feeling the flow of joyfulness is an indication that you are manifesting from the soul. There is a felt eagerness to move forward, a sense there is a higher purpose to whatever you do. When you notice that you have to force yourself to adopt a goal which really does not resonate, when each step is an effort and there is little joy in what you are doing, that is a clear indication you are manifesting from only the ego. This can happen when we only pay attention to what we want and ignore the signs and clues signaling where the flow is going and indicating what wants to happen. We have to take both personal desires and the needs of the greater whole into account.

There is nothing wrong with a strong ego. Indeed, it takes strength to put your ideas and goals out there and persist. To make our future brighter on this planet, we want strong egos informed with a greater perspective. We want to cultivate individuals who see the larger picture and who crave a world where each being is valued not for what it offers, but for its intrinsic place on the planet, its position in our delicate ecosphere.

We may agree to create something because we feel obligated or compelled. Sometime it sounds like we should want to do it. We may agree to step into the flow of someone else's creation while putting our own flow on a back burner. Sometimes that is alright. The back burner becomes a problem when you forget your life path and instead devote your energy to living someone else's dream.

Another reason we can be out of the flow is because we are trying to create out of fear. That is a big clue to *stop and pay attention*. Thoughts like these may be running through your mind: *"If I don't do this, then I will lose money!" "If I don't do this now, this opportunity will never come again!" "If I don't marry this person, no one else will ever love me!" "If I don't get this done right now, when will I ever do it? It will never get done."* Fear often leads us to a scarcity mentality and if we create out of scarcity, then we will reinforce scarcity in the world we are creating. Then there will be more scarcity and more fear of loss.

Think of it this way:

> Where there is fear, there can be no love.
> Where there is love there can be no fear.

It can be helpful to view fear and love as opposites. Next time you are faced with a dilemma, ask yourself, "Am I choosing based on fear or on love?"

Principle #3
How You Respond is Your Choice.

THOSE WHO CREATE take control of their moment. They do not allow anything (feelings, emotions, others' opinions, a bad day) to get in the way of their vision.

Remember Aron Ralston, the solo climber who in April 2003 was pinned by a huge boulder? Six days later, nearing death, with no help in sight and no hope of rescue, a powerful vision of his future self scooping up his three year old son moved him to take action and amputate his lower arm. He was able to walk to help, against all odds. Ralston spoke of the non-ordinary state of consciousness he entered as he decided to amputate his arm. *"It was strange. I kind of entered a flow state. I've been there before while climbing. You are not thinking ahead. You are just thinking about what is in front of you each second."*[10] This astonishing story of survival speaks to all of us as we contemplate how strong intention and desire inspired this man to make the fundamental choice for life.

Then there was "Miracle on Ice:" the 1980 Olympic US Hockey team. This team, assembled at the last minute, was made up of amateur and collegiate players. The Soviets were the heavy favorites and had won nearly every world championship and Olympic tournament since 1954. But this time it was the US team who took home the gold medal not because they were the most skilled but because they passionately believed in themselves and each other and because they were determined. They were very emotional about their performance: screaming, jumping up and down, laughing at their victories and crying at their losses. They rode to that medal on each others' enthusiasm and team spirit.

I know you have witnessed these types of scenes or something similar at some time in your life. Scenes when what seemed impossible to achieve became possible because of willpower, belief and persistence.

Now let's turn our attention back to you and what may be happening in your life. Consider these three different scenarios: *Distress, Contentment* and *Swept Away.*

> *Distress*: Do you find that when a difficult, stressful situation arises it tends to capture all of your attention, pulling your focus away from your goals? Think of a time when something really difficult happened that upended your entire life. Did you find yourself an unwilling rider on an emotional roller coaster? What emotions did you experience? How long did it take you to get over it? How far did you wander off from your true life purpose? How long did it take to get back your creative momentum?

Contentment: Now consider the other side of this equation. When things are going well for you, when things are just humming along and everything seems so easy, the promotions come, the love relationships are working out, and the finances are in place, do you forget your dreams of the future? Do you let them go? Does your contentment sap you of creative drive?

Swept Away by Outside Influences: Or here is another instance you may resonate to. When you have one of those amazing experiences like falling in love, winning big at a game of chance, coming into some money, or any time at all when unexpected good fortune comes your way, do you tend to give yourself over to that experience, getting swept away, ignoring the other important aspects of your life, putting your visions on the backburner, and losing focus on what is most important to you? As you think back on those positive experiences in your life, from this perspective of here and now, can you see how even the positive emotional experiences can distract you from your creative endeavors, from your purpose?

When emotions start to control us at the expense of our vision that is what I call emotional distress. It's not that emotions are bad. Quite the opposite, emotions are *essential* to the healthy well-functioning human being. But, emotional distress inhibits your ability to persist by causing you to back away from your dreams and settle for less.

You know what it feels like to be under emotional distress: sleepless nights, not wanting to get out of bed and face the day, upset stomachs, headaches, a mind preoccupied with trying to fix things, running over the same scenarios again and again until you have that haunted obsessive feeling. Emotional distress is discouraging.

Ask yourself these questions: Are you spending most of your life caught up in your emotions instead of bringing your dreams into reality? Are you working hard on your feelings, hoping someday you will be healed enough to move ahead? Do you put aside your dreams because you fear what others may think of you or because you doubt yourself? Or are you engaged in wishful thinking, hoping that someday something good is just going to descend upon you without you having to do anything about it, without you having to make any course corrections? Do you find yourself wishing and hoping things were different yet, at the same time, being reluctant or unsure with how to create the changes you want in your life?

One of the most important concepts you will learn here is that how you respond to your emotions and what you choose to do with them is your choice.

> Your emotions are not you. Your emotions are something that you choose to experience.

These emotions distract you from becoming the true architect of your life because they put the power to change and transform *outside* of you. Know this: nothing outside of you has any power to change you. All change comes from *within*.

Emotional distress inhibits your ability to persist by causing you to back away from your dreams and settle for less. Persistence is the key to manifesting whatever you truly want in your life.

Remaining persistent is challenging when you are being bombarded with guilt, shame, worry, fear and negative thinking. We have to return to being the architect of our lives instead of letting circumstance, others and emotions (theirs or ours) dictate our fortunes.

People who choose to become the architect of their lives are able to:

- ✧ Persist even when things don't go their way.
- ✧ Neutralize emotional distress that would stop others in their tracks.
- ✧ Tell the truth about what is happening in their here and now.
- ✧ Consistently clarify their vision.
- ✧ Absolutely trust the Co-Creative Process.

You may have noticed that sometimes creativity is enhanced by intense emotions. Let's examine this more closely by using anger as an example of intense emotions. We have all had the experience of feeling anger course through our veins. It's like having three extra espressos. You cannot help but leap into action! Yes, these emotions can be a short term solution leading to quick results, but anger by its very nature cannot create the kind of life that is fulfilling and joyful.

If you depend on anger as a motivating force for creating, then you will eventually realize that you are not creating what you had intended. When your mind is filled with anger, you will draw experiences that create yet more anger, pulling you even further away from who you are. You will be on an emotional roller coaster and will be drawn inexplicably closer to those very things you do not want in your life, repeating those same experiences over and over again, those very experiences you swore "I'll never do that again!" You are stuck in a pattern, continuing to manifest the same results over and over again. Furthermore, you will exhaust yourself with the intensity of this emotion.

> Using intense emotion to motivate yourself can be exhausting and certainly wastes energy you could be using to create.

I am not asking you to repress emotions; on the contrary, it is important to feel your feelings and express them responsibly. In the Co-Creative Process, you will learn to acknowledge your feelings and still move forward with your goals. Acknowledging your feelings is not necessarily acting on your feelings. The point is to learn how to respond to your emotions in a positive and direct way allowing you to become a more skillful and effective architect of your life.

Principle #4
Make the Fundamental Choice to be the Predominant Creative Force in Your Life.

WE ALL MAKE choices in our lives. Some choices are more important than others and some choices are so pivotal they influence other choices we make. Consciously prioritizing our choices helps us to stay focused on what is most important.

The fundamental choice rises above all other choices in importance and commits you to a basic life orientation (Fritz, 1989). There is no other choice that would ever trump a fundamental choice. Examples of fundamental choices are:

- ✧ you choose to be happy regardless of what is happening around you.
- ✧ you choose to be true to what is highest in you.
- ✧ you choose to be healthy.

A primary choice is a choice which supports the fundamental choice. For example, if happiness is one of your fundamental choices, then you might take time out from your usual routine to do something that reminds you of your choice to be happy. Or you might choose to be employed in a meaningful job thereby fulfilling your fundamental choice to create a purposeful life. Or you might choose to commit to a more healthful diet to support your fundamental choice to be healthy.

The secondary choice supports your primary choice. So a secondary choice might be to attend an aerobics class to support your primary choice of exercising regularly. Or it might be as simple as getting up earlier so you can get to work on time to support your primary choice to have a meaningful job. Or you might choose to shop for nourishing foods to support your primary choice to eat nourishing foods.

Figure One (below) demonstrates how secondary choices support primary choices which in turn support the fundamental choices.

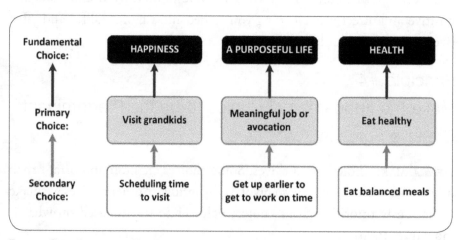

Figure One. Levels of Choices with Examples

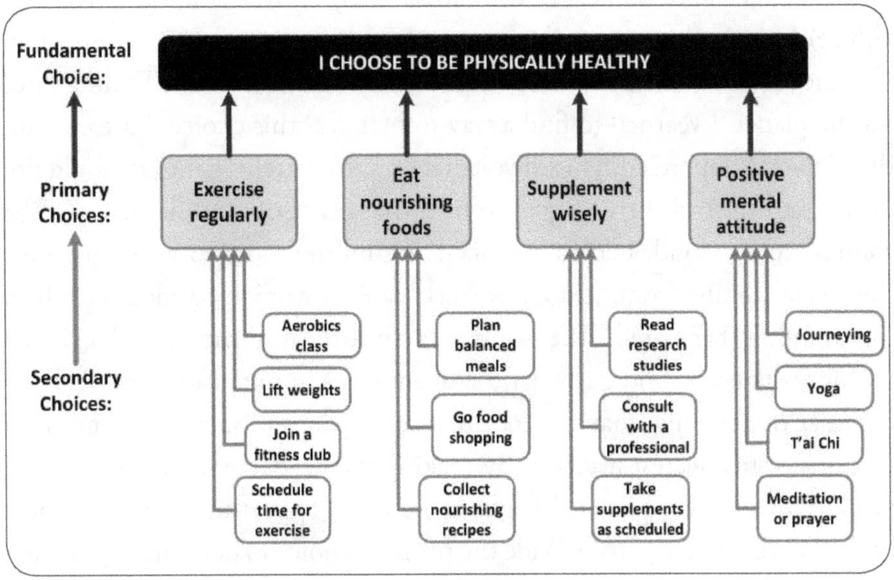
Fundamental Choice:
I CHOOSE TO BE PHYSICALLY HEALTHY
Primary Choices:
Exercise regularly
Eat nourishing foods
Supplement wisely
Positive mental attitude
Secondary Choices:
Aerobics class
Lift weights
Join a fitness club
Schedule time for exercise
Plan balanced meals
Go food shopping
Collect nourishing recipes
Read research studies
Consult with a professional
Take supplements as scheduled
Journeying
Yoga
T'ai Chi
Meditation or prayer

Figure Two. Flow Chart for One Fundamental Choice

Figure Two shows one fundamental choice and illustrates the many primary choices and even more numerous secondary choices that support one fundamental choice.

Fundamental choices, Fritz says, provide the foundation for primary and secondary choices. "When people make a fundamental choice to be true to what is highest in them, or when they make a choice to fulfill a purpose in their life, they can easily accomplish many changes that seemed impossible or improbable in the past."[11]

To become the Predominant Creative Force in your life, all of your primary and secondary choices must align with your fundamental choices. Here are some examples:

I have made the fundamental choice to be healthy, a choice I made in my early thirties. To support this fundamental choice, I have several primary choices: I exercise regularly, I eat nourishing foods, and I take supplements. My secondary choices naturally evolve from my primary choices. My secondary choices are to frequent an athletic club, buy organic foods, and stay on top of the latest research in supplementation. Clarity around my secondary choices makes other choices much easier. For example, once I have made a fundamental choice for health, I am not as likely to overeat foods (secondary choice) I know do not contribute to my health.

Another fundamental choice I made in my thirties is to be a healing force on the planet. I yearned to find a way to manifest this choice. Sure enough, the Universe responded. I heard voices several times telling me "it would not be long now." And then I began to hear the sound of a drum beating. The sounds were so loud, I actually looked around the room to find out where they were coming from. Just a few weeks later, a woman handed me a flyer to a training that stated "The drum is the heartbeat of the Earth." I signed up immediately to find out what the drum beats in my head were all about. It was at this training that the door to shamanism was opened for me and I met one of my dearest teachers. By making the fundamental choice to be a healing force on the planet, I began to be given opportunities to become a healer. Within a few years, I made the primary choice to dedicate my waking hours to healing and, as a result, I left my corporate job as an engineer.

Brandelyn R.[11] realized her fundamental choice is to bring music into her life at her very first Co-Creation class. In her own words,

> *Three years ago I attended Alida's Co-Creation course. On a small slip of paper I wrote down: I want to create a rock and roll band. At the time I had a guitar and some songs and really not much more in the way of music. Now, three years later I am a lead singer and guitar player in a touring rock and roll band named Blue Lotus.*

Once Brandelyn became clear on her primary choice, to manifest a rock and roll band, the Universe rapidly responded. Within a few months she had a gifted lead guitarist, songs spilling out of her soul, and bookings coming in. The demands of her day job prevented her from fully participating in her rapidly manifesting dream. Because she wanted to give more of her time to her music, she chose to shift to a more flexible less demanding job so she could fully focus on bringing music into her life, her fundamental choice. It wasn't always easy. She worked hard to support her two daughters, pay the bills, and juggle the demands of an active music career.

How else did the Universe respond to Brandelyn? Here are just a few of the ways I know of. A well-known celebrity photographer gifted her with a full day photo shoot. She had just written a local radio personality to see if she could get her music on his show. Then she met him by chance on a walk through a local park. The synchronicities didn't stop there. That evening, she found herself sitting next to him at a sold out concert. She took this opportunity to invite him to her band's performance that same night at a local nightclub. He accepted and after listening to her group, he offered to put her band on the radio.

When our fundamental, primary and secondary choices are clear, the Universe responds and synchronicities abound.

The Audio Program

THE AUDIO PROGRAM is available to you as an MP3 download from the website listed below. Click on the link for Audio. If you prefer to purchase a CD of the Audio Program, there are instructions on the website.

URL: www.Co-CreationHandbook.com
Password: hummingbird

The Audio Program is where the magic starts to happen. It is designed to take you through the Co-Creative Process step by step and is essential to mastering the skill of Co-Creation. The ability to manifest anything is greatly improved when you are in a non-ordinary state of consciousness because you will be aligning yourself with the Universal Powers. The intent of the Audio Program is to train you to enter into these non-ordinary states of consciousness. For this reason, the Audio Program is an essential part of this process.

There are many different ways to approach the wisdom, knowledge, and healing that are outside of our ordinary awareness and I have designed the Audio Program to introduce you to the methods I find most potent.

On the recording you will hear a steady drumbeat in the background. Shamans have used the drum for thousands of years to enter a type of meditative state called the shamanic state of consciousness. The sound of the drum has been proven to slow down the brainwaves to the theta state—the frequency of meditation.[12] Once in the theta state, shamans then choose to enter a non-ordinary reality. They do this to connect with loving and compassionate spirit beings who provide healing and wisdom to the shaman and their community.

> The shamanic journey is a time-tested doorway to enter the Spiritual Realms to solve problems and manifest well-being in the world.

Most people experience theta waves on their way to the delta state which produces sleep. So at first you may notice that you tend to fall asleep while listening to the Audio Program. For this reason, you may want to initially sit up while listening to the Audio Program to help you remain awake. Soon you will find yourself developing alertness while in the theta state. But if you do fall asleep while listening, be assured that your subconscious is still working with the visualizations. When you notice you've been asleep for a while, be grateful for the awareness that brought you back to waking consciousness and pick up where you left off.

You will be asking questions and receiving answers during some of the tracks. I do not define who you are interacting with during the questions, but leave that open for you to discover. Here are some of the possibilities. You may find an untapped source of wisdom, healing and knowledge. You may encounter Angels, God, the Divine, Saints, Goddesses, power animals, Infinite Mind, a primal substance, ancestors, deceased people, indescribable energies, forces of nature, the Void, and even yourself. Treat this as an experiment and an adventure. Come to this with a sense of wonder. See what emerges for you. Play with it. If you are surprised by what you encounter, know that you are in good company. A great many people over thousands of years have used these practices to expand their consciousness, seek advice, and develop new skills.

As you ask your questions, open up all of your senses so you can receive the answer. This may be something you can hear or see or taste or feel. Sometimes you will simply be infused with the answer you are seeking. Sometimes the answers will come during the pauses, but answers can also come to you later during the day or even in a dream. The answer may appear synchronistically to you within something someone says or an experience that you have.

> There is no wrong way to receive; however you receive is the perfect way for you.

As you ask the questions and receive answers, you will most likely struggle with the thought that you are imagining the answers and could not possibly be interacting with anyone other than yourself. This is a very common dilemma most westerners face when beginning shamanic journey training. To answer this, I will share with you what I have learned from my teachers about imagination.

There are many indigenous cultures that do not have a word for imagination in their vocabulary. Instead, when they experience thoughts which we westerners would define as coming from our imagination, they interpret this as being *inspired* and this is a critical difference. To be inspired means to be in-spirited, to be filled with the Spirits. The inference here is that all creative thought comes from the Spirits, not from our imagination. To these people, the imagination does not exist at all. When their mind is filled with a creative idea, they credit the Spirits for this inspiration. In their worldview, all creativity comes from the Spirits.

Most people tend to come out somewhere in the middle: most believe there is a Divine Spirit, some of us wonder if it speaks directly to us and many of us have been taught it does not speak to ordinary folk like you and me. So now I ask you to experiment with the idea that the Divine Beings and Helping Spirits will actually inform your thoughts if you ask them to. So as you ask your questions during these visualizations, welcome whatever thoughts come into your head as messages from the Spirits. Let go of any preconceived notions you may have about where inspiration comes from. Just for now, let go of beliefs that tell you this cannot be happening and it must be your imagination. Instead, think of your imagination as the doorway to the Spiritual Realms. Over time, as you work with this idea and allow yourself to become even more open to these new, deeper sources of knowledge and inspiration, you will be able to receive information and help when you call for it.

What if you call for help and it isn't there? First be patient and wait a few minutes for a response. If you still cannot discern a response, call on your imagination to make up a response. Eventually, like a rusty hinge receiving oil, your ability to access non-ordinary states will be enhanced and strengthened as you exercise your imagination. You will find at some point on your imagined journey, the storyline takes on a life of its own—not under your direct control. This means you have begun to journey.

Here is my story of how I struggled with this very same issue. I was called to the shamanic path in 1982. I had just moved to Green Bay Wisconsin and was working as a manufacturing engineer in a paper plant. I had great career opportunities yet I felt an emptiness inside me. I kept silently asking how I could find a greater purpose and I did not seem to be getting any answers. One day, quite unexpectedly, I began to hear a drumbeat in my head. It was a very steady repetitive beat with no syncopation. It just kept droning on and on. I got curious about it. To understand this, I felt I needed a drum and I started to ask other people if they had a drum I could borrow. I got some blank stares. At this time in the late 80's, I was not aware of anyone using a drum spiritually. I knew about bands and orchestras but not a spiritual use for the drum.

Then someone handed me a flier for a training entitled "The Shamanic Journey for Power and Healing." I did not know what shamanic meant. But I read through the flier and there it was in black and white: *The drum is the heartbeat of the earth.* I felt an odd sensation in my head. It seemed like the world receded and all that existed was that one phrase: *The drum is the heartbeat of the earth.* I felt compelled to attend this training and find out what this drumbeat in my head was all about. I promptly sent in my money but the weeks rolled by and I did not hear back from the organizer. I called the week before the training and the organizer told me he had not gotten my check and, sorry, but the training was full. I then blurted out I was supposed to be there. I could not believe those words had come out of my mouth. Even though I was standing alone in my kitchen, I turned bright red with embarrassment. It felt like something else was speaking through me. But then Myron Eschowsky, the organizer, very quickly and kindly said, "If you are supposed to be here, then we will make room."

So that Saturday I hopped into my car and drove the two and a half hours to Madison Wisconsin. I arrived five minutes before we were to start. I was told to sit down in the circle. People started drumming. Then, along with the steady drumbeat, people began to make cacophonous bird and animal calls. I began to wonder what I had gotten myself into. I wanted to leave.

I won't go into the details of the training but we did learn how to journey to the upper and lower worlds to meet our power animals and spiritual teachers. I was on the fence of doubt the entire time. I was well trained in the scientific method as an engineer. I have a Masters Degree in Social Work, which predisposed me to think we were really contacting our subconscious rather than actual spirits. I almost did not return to the second day of the training, but again something conspired to keep me there. A woman offered me a place to sleep at her home and it turned out she did not have a car. So I was obliged to bring her back to the training on Sunday and decided it made more sense to stay and finish out the weekend even though I was out of my comfort zone.

I remained on that fence of doubt for a year. I would journey but I would always doubt the source of the information I received. It was only when I took an advanced training in shamanic healing techniques and began to perform soul retrievals for others that I realized I was receiving details about my clients' lives and deepest issues that I had no logical access to. I was forced to acknowledge there was something beyond my subconscious at work. Even then, my very strong logical mind refused to accept these spiritual experiences as authentic. I finally had to realize my linear mind was trying to protect me and one day I said this to it:

Thank you for protecting and watching out for me. I understand your reservations. However, I also realize that you have disregarded some experiences that do not line up with your way of seeing the world. You in fact are lying to me. You are disregarding the results I and others are receiving through this work. I know you are trying to protect me. So I am going to put you over here in the corner for now. I will still take your advice into account but I will also listen to my Spirit Helpers and the voice of the Universe as it speaks to me in synchronicities, intuitions, and hunches and especially through the shamanic journey. And I will be the one to make a choice about which voices to follow and which path to take.

And to this day, I still have this conversation with my logical mind despite the amazing miracles I have seen with shamanic work. This logical part of me will never be convinced. That is OK. My logical mind helps me to walk in the ordinary world with great skill and helps me to know my boundaries. And this logical part helps me to teach others convincingly about this amazing technique called the shamanic journey.

More on How to Use the Audio Program

Expect long pauses during the narration. The recording is not malfunctioning. The pauses allow you to ask questions and receive answers. You will continue to hear the drumming during the pauses. If the answers are not coming immediately, simply listen to the drumming and trust that your mind is being prepared to receive the answer later when the time is right for you.

Each week's action steps will include listening to the Audio Program twice daily, once in the morning and once in the evening. Optimally, listen to the morning session as soon as you wake, and listen to the evening session just before closing your eyes to sleep. You might want to have the audio player sitting right on your bedside table. An eye covering may help you to focus more easily

Do not listen to the Audio Program while driving a vehicle or operating equipment.

The time you devote to the Audio Program is sacred time. It is the space you are creating twice each day to honor your vision for your life. You are welcoming in the Helping Spirits who will assist you in manifesting your dreams and creating an intentional life. It is a small investment compared to the changes you want. To honor this space, to honor you, and to honor the Helping Spirits, I have some suggestions for how you can create this sacred space.

Here are some ideas for you: light a candle, burn dried herbs such as sage or sweet grass and use the smoke as a smudge to clear the room and your aura. You may wish to play a crystal bowl if you have one or sound a bell. You can also tone or sing a simple song of thanks. If you are in a place where you are unable to use any of these methods, simply breathe deeply and focus your intention to honor the beings you are working with.

There are seven sets of visualizations which will take you through Week Seven. During Week Eight, in classic shamanic journey style, you will be journeying to the drum without any prompting from my voice.

For Week One, the Audio Program will assist you in making the fundamental choice to be happy, acknowledging your feelings and moving forward with your goals.

Action Steps: Week One

- Choose a small goal that you would like to work on this week. Make it something that is fairly easy to accomplish, not emotionally loaded, perhaps something you have been procrastinating on. Pick a goal that is fairly new for you, perhaps a new project or interest you would like to develop. It can be as simple as planting a garden, organizing a shelf, cleaning your room, or reading a book. Write your small goal down on a piece of paper. Also write down a description of three scenes with your goal accomplished. For example, if your goal is to read a book, you might imagine in one scene that you are turning the last page and closing the book. In another scene, you might see yourself putting the book away on a shelf. In a third scene you might hear yourself discussing the book with a friend. You will need to have your goal and three scenes for Week One of the Audio Program.

- If you complete the goal before the end of the week, choose another goal to work with.

- Download the Audio Program from www.Co-CreationHandbook.com, password: hummingbird

- Every morning and evening for the next eight weeks, start and end your day by listening to the Audio Program. This week use the tracks for Week One which are "Week One AM" and "Week One PM." Make that commitment now. Schedule it into your day and start today.

- Start a journal. Each day, write down five things you are grateful for.

How to Vision

Your vision will become clear only when you look into your heart.
Who looks outside, dreams. Who looks inside, awakens.

—C. G. Jung

As WE CO-CREATE, there are three skills to master

- ❖ Manifesting: learning and integrating the skills of creating.
- ❖ Developing Flow: recognizing that the inner flow of truth is an indication your soul is in harmony with what you are creating.
- ❖ Co-Creating: enlisting the help and counsel of spiritual beings to bring forth those creations you wish to manifest.

In the natural world everything is a circle. When we acknowledge this and look for them, we can see circles everywhere: the tree trunk grows in concentric circles, birds build their nests in circles, some native peoples build their houses in circles, and the earth herself is a circle, albeit a three dimensional one. From shamanism we learn that all beings have a place within the circle and each has a significant role to play, important skills to share and critical pieces of the puzzle to contribute.

In our study of co-creation, the circle is a very useful concept. Energy flows in circles. From the circle we learn that everything we send out flows back to us. We work with what has returned and send it out again. This cycle is the flow of life we are all a part of.

As we learn to co-create, we use intention to skillfully shift that flow for the benefit of all beings.

> The importance of the circle in shamanic practice speaks to the understanding that each member of the circle has a unique contribution to make to the whole. If this contribution does not come forth, the circle suffers and is not complete. As our global consciousness increases and we realize that we are all accountable for the health of our planet, we realize that we must have a planetary consciousness and our ethics must now encompass planetary ethics.
>
> You are a part of this larger planetary circle. The personal and the planetary are connected. You are an expression of the Divine and have a contribution to make. Without you the circle is broken.

I respect who you are as an expression of the Divine and that is why I am encouraging you to allow your uniqueness to manifest so you may share your talents and gifts. It is truly a joyful experience to be able to bring your talents and gifts forward. Creating and moving towards your vision is truly an expression of your soul.

This is your sacred and collaborative adventure with the Divine.

Merriam-Webster.com defines *manifestation* as "a perceptible, outward, or visible expression." As I use the word manifestation here, it is to describe an outward expression of the soul—the soul being our essence or, in other words, our vital life force. Your essence is unique to you alone—no one else sees what you see or hears exactly what you hear or feels what you are feeling. No one else has exactly the same gifts and talents you have. Manifestation is about using your unique gifts and talents to bring forth those creations that are a direct expression of all you hold to be most precious.

Let's take a step back to get a bigger perspective of our world. Probably you have noticed there are monumental problems of global warming, over-population, political conflict, depletion of resources, violence and world hunger. This all seems like an overwhelming, unsolvable puzzle.

I do not believe our world problems are unsolvable. Rather, I believe each and every one of us holds a small but essential piece of the puzzle. If each one of us is fully stepping into our greatness and is shown a way to manifest our unique gifts and talents, we will be able to create a self-sustaining world with enough for every being on the planet. We will be able to create a future we would want ourselves and our descendants to live in, a future we can be proud of. The changes we need for this global transformation to succeed will happen from the bottom up, one person at a time.

Once you have mastered the Co-Creation Process, you will find you are able to directly contribute to the creation of an abundant, peaceful world for future generations.

Visioning from the Ground Up

All cultures respect the importance of vision and its capacity to magnetize, or open up, the creative spirit.

—Angeles Arrien

THE KEY TO success with manifesting is the vision. A vision gives you direction and focus, anchoring you in the future, pulling you to your goal.

Before we dive into the visioning process, a word of reassurance here. Are you one of those people whose mind goes blank when asked specifically what it is you want to manifest? Maybe the idea of imagining a vision is overwhelming or the word 'vision' seems so lofty you cannot see its relevance in your life. Are you finding that the word *vision* is a stumbling block for you? If so, I invite you to work indirectly with your subconscious and reframe the word *vision* with a substitute word that may work better for you.

One way to do this is to choose another word which serves the same purpose as *vision*. If your mind has difficulty with the word *vision*, substitute the word *intention*. When you examine the word *intention*, you discover that it means the tension you hold inwardly. Intention is the inner tension between who you are and who you are becoming. Ask *what is my intention?* instead of *what is my vision?* Does that help?

Or you can simply ask: *What do I want in my life?*

Now let's cover some basic groundwork.

Do not limit your vision by what you think is possible.

Many inventors are able to create because they do not realize what they are envisioning is considered by others to be impossible. Truly creative people are able to create because they simply assume their vision is absolutely possible.

In 1961, John F. Kennedy gave a famous speech in which he challenged America to send a man to the moon by the end of the decade. Most people seriously doubted that would ever happen, but his dream was achieved on July 20, 1969.

Just last week in my local paper, I spotted an article about the development of a bionic eye that gives sight to the blind. While this is groundbreaking and exciting news, what really caught my attention was the comment of the chief executive, Robert Greenburg, who got tired of hearing from senior engineers that it wasn't possible to build his product idea. "A lot of folks straight out of school didn't know any better, so I hired them instead." Called the Argus II Retinal Prosthesis System, the device recently was approved by the Food and Drug Administration.[13]

In 2002, I was living in the small city of Eugene, Oregon. I wanted to live in the country but my husband was devoted to city life. He told me he had no intention of moving out of the city. I knew in my heart that once he experienced country living, he would love it. So I began to envision our house in the country. Soon, much to his surprise, he was accompanying me on house showings. He began to remember a childhood dream of having his own vineyard. Even though we had a realtor looking for our house, I spent every free moment searching for our house on my own. I was convinced I could manifest this house through sheer willpower and lots of activity. Nothing was happening and I was really becoming exhausted. Finally I reeled myself in and chose to work with the visioning process. I clarified my vision, felt joy and passion in anticipation of the vision becoming my reality, and then I let it go. I gave my vision over to the Divine. Then the realtor began pestering me to visit a house we had already seen and rejected. She insisted that we take another look. Reluctantly, we agreed. It was perfect. It had the potential garden and vineyard, the woods, the pond, a large space for our trainings and workshops, a place for the cats and bees, and more. It was everything we had asked for! I just hadn't seen it clearly before because I wasn't clear on my vision. I had tried to force it to happen through sheer willpower and activity. I had not given the Divine permission to co-create with me.

Becoming Conscious of Your Vision

MOST PEOPLE ARE not conscious of what they are creating in their life. They get so caught up in the daily grind that they forget there could be more meaning, more happiness, and more abundance in their lives.

> The truth is we are creating all of the time, but we are doing it unconsciously.

A vital step is to become conscious of what we are creating. The bigger or more important the vision, the more effort you will want to put into clarifying exactly what your vision is.

Here are some tips for consciously creating a vision or intention that I will expand on in the next several pages.

- ⬧ You can begin by looking at what you don't want in your life and substitute a positive replacement you really do want. Or you can identify what is really important to you and connect that to what you will create in your life.
- ⬧ To keep yourself on track, ask: "When I obtain this vision, is this something I really want? What is it for? What is its purpose? How will my life change when I achieve this vision? What will my life be like 5 years from now as I continue to create this vision?" Asking yourself these questions is helpful in taking charge and focusing in on what you really want to create in your life.
- ⬧ What you absolutely need to know about your vision is this: your vision springs from your imagination. This means *you get to make it up*. This is a great secret of creative people. In this first step of visioning, use your imagination to create an intention. Knowing this frees you to create whatever vision feels right to you. You are not limited by current circumstances. And you do not have to have the whole

picture in front of you before you start to formulate a vision. It's okay if you don't yet know the details. In fact, not knowing the details is preferable.

♦ If you find your mind goes blank as you stare at the paper, I invite you to relax and then give yourself the suggestion that the intention will come to you somewhere as you go about your day. Recall from Week One when we learned that inspiration can be viewed as coming from the Divine.

♦ It's okay if you don't know what you want to be when you grow up or what you want to do for a living. It's even okay if you have no idea what you want to do with the day in front of you. You may have let other people decide what you should do, what you think about and how you are supposed to feel. If so, then think of visioning as a new skill you are learning: to think for yourself, to feel your own feelings, to do things for yourself and to collaborate with the Divine. Give it some time and effort, step by step. I promise you: it's worth it.

What is important is to always remember to take the next step: you can make a plan, you can come up with a vision and you can bring that vision into reality. And if those are missing for you, make it up. Go ahead and take the next step – even if it's a baby step. This gets you moving and, as we will see later, movement is essential. It's like raising the sails on your sailboat. The winds of creativity may be blowing strong in your direction, but if you don't raise your sails you will just sit there dead in the water.

If you are someone who is not used to making choices or if you tend to go along with what everyone else wants, you may find the idea of choosing your own goal to be difficult. You may have to sit quietly by yourself in order to think clearly about what you want.

If you find that fear stops you, if you find yourself worrying about worst case scenarios, I have a suggestion for you: *spend time clarifying your vision*. The clearer you get on your vision, the easier it will be to move towards it and through any obstacles that may come up along the way.

If you find yourself endlessly going over and over and over how you are going to achieve your vision *that* is your ego banging its head against the wall. This is exactly the moment when you will need to let go of how you think it is going to work and give your vision over to the Universe.

We will cover how to give your vision over to the Universe in the Audio Program.

Here is a simple example of taking a risk with visioning in an area I was not having success:

In 1986, I was in my early 30s, sedentary, working 60 hours a week and finding lots of excuses not to exercise. I wanted to run but running was painful for me. I strained to run two miles; my lungs felt like they would burst. I thought this dream was impossible.

It took a management meeting at work to spark a small miracle in my life. Of course, I could not see it then because I just thought I was being roped into something I would fail at. At the meeting, the managers were encouraged to run a ten kilometer race in six months for charity. To my dismay, peer pressure won out: everyone signed up, even me.

How could I get myself through that six plus mile race with dignity and any chance of finishing?

Out of desperation, I called my friend, Monica, an avid runner who loves to race. She advised me on resources, encouraging me to join the running club and to read books about racing. As the weeks went on, I stuck with it. I kept visualizing myself at that finish line. As I had success with my running workouts, I reasoned I could do triathlons because I already knew how to swim and bicycle. I had not yet finished my first 10k race but I was already visioning my next step: the triathlon. I wasn't a natural athlete, I didn't win any races, but I had some results I was proud of. I finished several 10k races. The next summer, I finished two triathlons. And to this day, these memories are some of my favorites.

Here are the important points of my story:

- ⋄ I had no idea how I was going to accomplish it
- ⋄ I set my vision based on what I wanted, *not* what I thought was possible
- ⋄ The Universe found a way to get me committed
- ⋄ I moved from panic to excited expectation

- ✧ I reached out for resources (Monica, the running club)
- ✧ I used momentum (studying, planning, small steps, joining with others)
- ✧ I set a new bigger vision that helped me push beyond my original vision

I will now lead you through a process to help you set a vision or intention quickly and easily. We will start with past successes.

Visioning Successes

LET'S START BY thinking about some of the successes you have already had with visioning. Substitute the word *intention* or *reaching your goal* if the word *vision* is too big. Jot the successes down below as they occur to you. Put down some small ones and some big ones too.

Two examples are:
- ✧ I got a job
- ✧ I finished a challenging class

NOW WRITE DOWN YOUR SUCCESSES IN THE AREA BELOW:

_____

_____

_____

_____

_____

_____

_____

_____

Identifying the five major areas in your life

IT IS HELPFUL to start the visioning process by thinking about and identifying your intentions in these five areas of your life:

- ✧ Abundance
- ✧ Appearance
- ✧ Health
- ✧ Work and Projects
- ✧ Relationships

Now make a list of goals for yourself in these five areas. Remember, it is not about what you think is possible. It is about choosing to create something that you want. Take a risk. You are brainstorming now, so very quickly and without thinking about it too much, make a few notes next to each category. If you knew you could accomplish anything you set out to do, what would you like to bring forth in these areas?

GOALS FOR THE FIVE MAJOR AREAS

Relationships _____

_____

Health _____

_____

Work/Projects _____

_____

Appearance _____

_____

Abundance _____

_____

Now, review each goal and ask yourself if you feel a sense of joy and excited anticipation at the thought of this goal completed. If not, go back and ask yourself if this goal is really something you choose, something you really want in your life. If the answer is yes, is the goal clear enough, is it big enough?

Here is an example of a goal focused on abundance:

Bonnie P. chose to have her dream bicycle. She did not have the money to purchase the bicycle. She used the method of clarifying what she wanted, noticing that she did not have the bike, and feeling the creative tension between her goal and her current reality. She then released her desire to the Divine. A local store advertised the bike as a lottery prize. She didn't win. She kept on. Within a few weeks, she received a large sum of money unexpectedly. She immediately thanked the Divine (yes!) and purchased the bike. When she is not riding the bike, she has placed it in her living room where she often notices it and feels grateful for this wonderful manifestation of her goal.

ALTERNATE PATH

If you have difficulty with generating ideas in any area, try this instead: make a list of things you do not like about your current situation. Once you've made a list of what you don't want, draw a line through each of those items and put an arrow in front of it pointing to the right column. In front of this arrow, write down what you would like to manifest instead. See the example below.

Going back to my example about running the 10k race:

My current reality	What I choose to manifest
~~I am not physically fit~~ ->	To be physically fit

Now go ahead and make your list.

TURNING WHAT YOU DON'T WANT INTO WHAT YOU CHOOSE TO MANIFEST

My current reality	What I choose to manifest

Relationships _____

_____

Health   _____

_____

Work/Projects _____

_____

Appearance   _____

_____

Abundance   _____

_____

Now integrate the two lists you have already completed by taking those items from your two lists under **Goals for the Five Major Areas** on page 41 and **Turning What You Don't Want into What You Choose to Manifest** on page 42 and consolidate your favorite ones under **What I Choose to Manifest** (below). Then break these choices down further into smaller steps. I call this the *chunking down* process.

To continue with my example of being physically fit, smaller steps would be: to run twice a week; eat nourishing foods; and run a 10k race.

Major Area: Health (*example*)	
What I choose to manifest (1):	*Smaller steps*
Good Physical Fitness	a. **Run twice a week**
	b. **Eat nourishing foods**
	c. **Run a 10k race**

Major Area: Relationships	
What I choose to manifest (1):	*Smaller steps*
	a.
	b.
	c.
What I choose to manifest (2):	*Smaller steps*
	a.
	b.
	c.
What I choose to manifest (3):	*Smaller steps*
	a.
	b.
	c.

Major Area: Health	
What I choose to manifest (1):	*Smaller steps*
	a.
	b.
	c.
What I choose to manifest (2):	*Smaller steps*
	a.
	b.
	c.
What I choose to manifest (3):	*Smaller steps*
	a.
	b.
	c.

Major Area: Work/Projects	
What I choose to manifest (1):	*Smaller steps*
	a.
	b.
	c.
What I choose to manifest (2):	*Smaller steps*
	a.
	b.
	c.
What I choose to manifest (3):	*Smaller steps*
	a.
	b.
	c.

Major Area: Appearance	
What I choose to manifest (1):	*Smaller steps*
	a.
	b.
	c.
What I choose to manifest (2):	*Smaller steps*
	a.
	b.
	c.
What I choose to manifest (3):	*Smaller steps*
	a.
	b.
	c.

Major Area: Abundance		
What I choose to manifest (1):	Smaller steps	
	a.	
	b.	
	c.	
What I choose to manifest (2):	Smaller steps	
	a.	
	b.	
	c.	
What I choose to manifest (3):	Smaller steps	
	a.	
	b.	
	c.	

Now we will keep chunking it down by taking those smaller steps and breaking it down even further. Here's an example using the 10k race: a smaller goal would be to run two miles three times a week:

Run a 10k race ————————> **Run two miles three times a week**

Now from the above list pick out some *smaller steps* you want to focus on and rewrite them on the next page. This now becomes your *Things I Choose to Manifest* list. When you have several smaller steps for each broader category we can go on to the next step. This is the heart of visioning so spend some time creating this list.

THINGS I CHOOSE TO MANIFEST:

_____

_____

_____

_____

_____

_____

_____

_____

_____

_____

_____

_____

_____

_____

_____

_____

The Stretch Goal

> The purpose of the stretch goal is to begin training your subconscious to manifest what <u>you choose</u>.

THE NEXT STEP is called the stretch goal. This is a small goal you choose to work with that will help you to re-train your subconscious. This is a relatively *minor* goal in the scheme of your life. It is not a big emotional goal with huge ramifications (such as weight loss, getting married, making more money, or getting promoted) nor is it a goal which calls deeply to your meaning and purpose. Make sure it is a goal you have *not* worked with before. The stretch goal for you is no big deal. You won't be terribly disappointed if it doesn't come to pass; neither will you be exhilarated if it does.

The stretch goal should have some great possibilities for movement. When you visualize the stretch goal, do you feel inspired? Are you eager to take the next step? Can you sense lots of ideas for moving forward? Do you feel a flow towards the stretch goal that is compelling?

The stretch goal is something so concrete there will be an easy way to measure its accomplishment, such as *plant 200 daffodil bulbs* or *identify the perfect contractor for the kitchen remodel*. If you have a generalized goal such as *increase my productivity at work*, you must also have a concrete way to track it.

You do need to be able to answer these questions:

How will you know when you get it?

How will you know when it is accomplished?

For example, if your goal is to have a clean car, you will know you have accomplished this goal when you look at the car and there is no dirt on or in the car, the windows are clean, the trash is gone from the inside, and it is polished Then you can stand back and say "Wow, this is a clean car!"

The more detail around the finished product, the greater the clarity of your vision. And this detail will pull you more towards completion, creating that flow.

My first ever stretch goal was to have a year-round dry basement in my house at a bargain price. I lived on the shore of a large body of water so this was a challenge and, as a new homeowner, I had no idea how to accomplish this without spending lots of money.

So now pick *one* of your goals as your stretch goal and write it here:

_____

_____

_____

And then add how you will know when you get it:

_____

_____

_____

Pssst: I know you want to get started on those big important items on your list. I assure you, as you are training with the stretch goal, you will automatically begin to manifest on all levels with your other intentions. Take a baby step here and trust the process. Stick with one stretch goal that is not of huge importance to your life.

Now that you have your list made up and your stretch goal chosen, you are thinking YES, I am going to make these things HAPPEN!!!

I now ask you not to get overly attached to your list. Even if you think your list and your stretch goal is the stuff of pure genius.

Here are two reasons why it is important that you do not get attached to specific outcomes:

You have identified what you think will be best for you. What you do not have access to is knowing what the Universe has planned for you. You do not know that once you begin to hold your vision in your mind and tell the truth about your observable present, things will start to line up for you in amazingly synchronistic and unusual ways. Ways that *you* could never have thought of.

> Staying in a state of not knowing allows the Universe to continue to play around on your behalf and eventually provide you with the perfect option.

People will show up in your life. Resources will become available. All you have to do is to allow all possibilities to unfold. Remember to continue to be in awe of what is transpiring for you. There may be something far better coming down the pike and you don't want to ignore it because it is not exactly what you had on your list. So yes, get your goals and visions out there and move toward them. But be prepared for tap dancing lessons from God, the Goddess, spirit, or your higher power. They may decide to send you down a different path. That's alright; it does not mean you are a failure. Simply adjust. You may encounter strange yet meaningful "coincidences." You may meet amazing and wonderful people who will help make your visionings come true and they may even help you to have bigger and better dreams. So stay flexible.

> Focusing on the destination is much more powerful than focusing on all the steps between you and your vision.

There's a key difference between knowing your destination and knowing the path. What is the quality you are after? Is it the eight person Jacuzzi tub and the fourteen raised garden beds or is it a place where you can feel at home, at peace and connected to the earth? If you rigidly attach to the "how's" and the "what's" you will find yourself getting more involved in the details and you may miss the opportunity to notice something that gets you closer to your vision. Why does this work? Because when you back away from the controls, the possibilities stay in play until the optimum pathway emerges. Remember that your perspective is limited; there may be a far better outcome waiting for you if you stay open to the possibilities.

I learned this lesson when I put in an order for a stable loving relationship. I was very specific (that's good.) However, when he showed up, I didn't recognize him because he did not fit all the criteria I had set (and I had quite the list). Since I had attached to the specifics and I was confident the Universe would send me the perfect man, I told him to go away. Thankfully he persisted and several months later the light bulb went on for me. I finally realized he was so much more than I had asked for. This year we celebrate 21 years together. This is why I am so adamant about this lesson: don't attach to the specifics in terms of how you get there.

The second reason to stay emotionally detached from your goals is to reduce *distress*. You can reduce distress by instead focusing on a different type of stress called *creative tension*. This key concept is fundamental to your ability to manifest.

Telling the truth about your observable present exactly as it is in the here and now is critical to reaching your goals. Your observable present is, very simply, what you have, who you are being in the world and what you are experiencing now. Notice the word 'observable.' When we observe something, we notice all we are capable of comprehending in the present moment. Our observations are limited by our past experiences and what we believe to be possible.

Our observations of our observable present are in no way the complete picture of *what is*. In *Stranger in a Strange Land*, Robert Heinlein introduces the concept of Fair Witness as one who is trained to be impartial and accurate. A Fair Witness is an individual trained to observe events and report exactly what he or she sees and hears, making no extrapolations or assumptions. For example, a character in the book is asked to describe the color of a house seen in the distance. The character responds, "It's white on this side" whereupon it is explained that one would not assume knowledge of the color of the other sides of the house without being able to see them. Furthermore, after observing another side of the house, one should not then assume that any previously seen side was still the same color as last reported, even if only minutes before.

While being a Fair Witness is not possible for many of us, I do hold it as a goal for myself to be more discerning and perceptive about what is really going on in my observable present and separating out my assumptions.

Telling the truth about what is really happening in your life can cause some discomfort. Sometimes with a jolt we discover the truth about our observable present. Personally, I have experienced times when my observable present was so contracted that I was completely oblivious to what I was unconsciously creating. Maybe it was a friend who stopped by and said "Do you really see what you are settling for? Is this what you want?" that allowed me to be completely honest about my current situation. Maybe I caught myself pondering "*why* I couldn't do something" when the real question is "*how* can I do it?" For example, I am reminded of how my observable present does not focus on the improvement of my home. I tend to be blocked when thinking about how my home could be different or better for me. When I finally focus on remodeling a room usually with the help of someone who has the skills I lack, I am stunned at all the wonderful possibilities. As I visualize the room as it could be and then I notice how it is, amazing energy is unleashed. That is what we call excited expectancy. When I see the vision, I feel compelled to do something about it. The discomfort generated by telling the truth about the present moment is rapidly replaced by excited expectation.

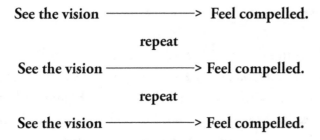

See the vision ⸺⸺⸺> Feel compelled.

repeat

See the vision ⸺⸺⸺> Feel compelled.

repeat

See the vision ⸺⸺⸺> Feel compelled.

Repeatedly focusing on the vision will compel you to move towards it.

Finding Courage

You may find yourself ambling down a career path and then suddenly notice that you are not sure how you got there. Amid the hustle and bustle of deciding on a career, you may have forgotten your vision for your life and put aside what you know to be your natural gifts. And at a deeper level, there is a profound forgetfulness or numbness that is engrained in us from our culture: a socialization that causes us to forget our own true nature, the calling of our soul, and a way to live out of the box which society would like us to live in.

How do we find the courage to tell the truth about ourselves and our world when we have been living so long in a world of half truths and deception? Start with loving compassion for yourself. This means releasing judgment. This means knowing in your heart that you are searching for the truth of who you are and what you want to create even if it feels far away and unattainable right now, *even if you have disappointed yourself in the past.* For this moment, right now, be compassionate and gentle with yourself.

And start to be curious about what you are observing in your present moment. Allow your curiosity to be greater and more intriguing than the fear of failure. Allow your curiosity to be greater than the anger and the disappointment. Feed your curiosity.

I find curiosity to be a wonderful tool for moving past fear.

If I can wonder:

- *How might this happen?*
- *What can I do to contribute to this?*
- *What is it that I really want in this situation?*

Then I am much more able to disengage from the many fears that accompany change.

Courage is not a lack of fear. It may be that as long as we are in a physical body hardwired for fear we will always have fear. Fear without courage will almost certainly lead to failure. But fear with courage will lead to change. Many of those who perform courageous feats will say that they were terrified but still chose to move forward. They realized that what they wanted to do was more important than their fear, more important than staying in the same place.

This is why it is so critical to come to terms with what *you* will take a stand for. We all will be faced with moments in our lives when we have to choose whether to succumb to fear or whether to move forward into uncertain territory. You must prepare for those moments by knowing what you stand for, what your values are, and what is so important to you that you will not back down. As Audre Lorde so eloquently commented, "When I dare to be powerful, to use my strength in the service of my vision, then it becomes less and less important whether I am afraid."

The Observable Present, Distress, and Creative Tension

Creative tension emerges when you clarify your vision, tell the truth about what is going on right now, and notice the difference between the vision and your observable present. Creative tension is moderate or normal psychological stress interpreted as being beneficial for the experience.

CREATIVE TENSION IS the dissonance between what is and what can be. Creative tension is the result of noticing that your vision and your observable present do not match. It is a helpful and necessary byproduct of visioning. It does not produce emotional distress because it does not contain judgment. It is evoked by simply noticing what is true and what you choose to create. Creative tension builds on Fritz's concept of structural tension[2] that creates a drive toward the vision and adds a connection to spiritual or universal power that provides powerful extraordinary resources.

To create creative tension, you will examine your life from the standpoint of your observable present *and* what you are choosing to manifest in your life.

What is true for you at the present moment is your observable present. And then there is the vision that is your desired future. Noticing the gap between the two is what propels you to your vision.

> In order to generate creative tension, you need to notice 3 things:
> - your observable present
> - your vision
> - creative tension = the difference between the two

Any system under stress wants to lessen the stress and will do so by one of two ways.

Ideally, (and this is most desirable) the observable present will move towards the vision. This is making progress towards the vision.

Observable present ————> **Vision**

Alternatively, the vision becomes compromised and will move back towards the observable present.

Observable present <——————— Vision

This is compromising your vision (also called "giving up" or "giving in.") This is not desirable and often happens when the vision is perceived to be too difficult or there is distress.

Many people will compromise on their vision by deciding their observable present is enough. You've heard them say it; you've probably heard yourself say it: "This isn't so bad; maybe I should give up on my dreams." Many are afraid to think big. Many are afraid to think of how their life could be different. Others compromise their vision due to pressure from the outside world, peers, friends, family, co-workers, even teachers.

Here is an example of how the manifestation steps work:

- Joe wants a home with a swimming pool for the kids (*vision*).

- Joe's *observable present* is:
  - renting a 2 bedroom duplex,
  - has two kids age 9 and 10,
  - saving $100 per month, married,
  - savings of $1500, working at job for 2.5 years, excellent credit history.

The vision is a description of what Joe wants, in this case a home with a swimming pool for the kids. Other descriptions of the house that he could bring in: color, size, neighborhood, schools, size of pool, who lives in the house with him and the kids, is there a BBQ, are there lots of kids in the neighborhood for his kids to play with, is there a car in the driveway (what kind), are the neighbors friendly?

To vision most effectively, you want to be able to see it, feel it, smell it, hear it, and know it. Incorporating the different senses is helpful because this brings the visioning process into the physical body. It becomes an experience rather than just a thought process. Purposefully opening up all of your senses to describe a vision is a skill you will develop and you will do this in the Audio Program. And finally, you must tap into your passion. Why is your vision important to you? How does it align with your deeper values? What is the underlying feeling as you focus on your vision?

Imagine how your life will be in six months, one year, and five years as your vision manifests.

Joe might draw a picture of how he wants the house to appear, he might imagine the neighborhood sounds from his backyard, the feeling on his skin as he dives into the pool, and the look on his wife's face as the realtor hands him the key to the front door. *Even more important* is that he notices how he *feels* as he creates the picture of the new house, as he hears the neighborhood sounds, the splash in his backyard pool and the look on his wife's face as he receives the house key.

> As you are creating the details of your vision, remember that the details are useful only in that they give you something to focus on. Do not attach to these details. Instead attach to the deeper values that the vision represents. What is the underlying feeling as you see your vision become manifest?

In Joe's case, those values might be creating a happy childhood for his children. Yet, as a skilled manifestor, he will remember there are multiple ways to create happy childhoods: buying a house with a swing set, a yard to play in, an atmosphere of love and acceptance, and a pool is just one way. But his vision would be equally satisfied by renting a duplex with a park next door that contained a play yard, a pool, and is in a family oriented neighborhood with great schools. What is important for Joe is that he creates a vision based on his values and he uses that vision to generate creative tension. He also needs to pay attention to what the Universe is sending his way that would also completely satisfy his vision and values.

Joe understands that successful manifestors do not attach to the details but do attach to the vision. The duplex he finally rents near the swim center and park is a success. His values for his family are met. In his visioning process he developed details to help propel himself towards the vision even if the outcome is different than his details of his vision. He reached his vision and that is what is important.

Here's another example: Sally C. needed a roof for her greenhouse. She visualized someone giving her the roof and felt satisfaction and pleasure as she enjoyed her greenhouse. But when an unexpected payment from an insurance company arrived in the mail that also satisfied her vision because she was now able to buy the roof and enjoy her greenhouse in the way she envisioned it.

Stay focused on your desired end result, filling yourself with all the feelings, emotions, and passion, and do not get attached to specifically how your end result comes to be.

When you focus on the observable present and the vision *simultaneously*, creative tension is generated. You then evoke something that is so magical it stimulates and brings forth something else that propels you towards your vision.

This is excited expectancy.

More on Distress and Excited Expectancy

So HOW DO you generate creative tension yet not allow it to move into the dreaded realm of distress? Give the process over to something greater than you. You may characterize this as God, the Divine, Source, the Helping Spirits, the Universe, a higher power, or the Great Mystery. If you are an atheist, just imagine throwing it out into a void of emptiness or into a great soup of possibilities.

The important point here is you let it go and give the process over.

Remember your stretch goal? One of the criteria for picking it was that it was not to be important. As you begin to expand your visioning capacity, it is necessary for you to firmly anchor this concept of letting go of the outcome. Even though it is important to you, you are not attached to it. You are not attached to the specific outcome because you trust that, in this co-creative relationship between you and the Divine, something is coming your way that will fulfill your vision and it may not be in the way you expect.

One way to let the specifics go is to create a ceremony around your vision. Ceremonies are perfect ways to engage the body, mind, and spirit. And ceremonies are a way to announce to the Universe the importance of your vision with great intention. The end result of the ceremony is that you hand the process over to the powers of manifestation.

The Burning Bowl Ceremony[14]

Here is one of my favorite simple ceremonies for setting intention.

In this ceremony, you will create an object that represents your vision. Then with your intention you will ask the object to become filled with the spirit of your vision. Finally, you will offer this vision now in concrete form to the fire so it may be transformed into the realms of manifestation.

1. Set your vision, what you would like to manifest? You may write this on a scrap of paper. Or you may hold this vision in your mind as you craft something to hold the intention. Examples are a stick wrapped with multi-colored strings, a small boat made from twigs, a small acorn on a leaf or a piece of paper with a statement of your vision. This will be burned so please use natural materials that burn well but nothing so large that it may burn out of control.

2. As you light a fire (a candle, a fireplace or small fire in a bowl if inside or a fire pit if outside), ask the spirit that fuels this fire to be one of manifestation. Bring some sage, tobacco or cedar to offer to the fire spirit as gratitude for the help it is giving to you. Always be safe and have a source of water available to douse the fire if needed.

3. Bring your attention to your object. Contemplate your vision, what you wish to manifest. Observe your observable present. What is happening now? Again revisit the vision. Notice the creative tension. Feel the excited expectancy. Spend as much time here as you need to fully embody these thoughts and emotions. Ask that this intention move fully into the object; feel it come alive, taking on the spirit of your intention.

4. When you feel the intention is as much in the object as possible, release the object into the flame with these words: "Please take this intention into the realm of manifestation." Watch as the flame devours your object, bringing your intention fully into the realm of Spirit. Trust that the Divine is now fully engaged on your behalf.

5. You may wish to dance and sing as you release this intention to the Divine. Thank the fire by feeding it with the sage, tobacco or cedar. You may be inspired to sing songs and chants of gratitude to the spirit of the fire and the Divine Beings watching over your ceremony.

6. If possible, watch as the fire burns out naturally. Otherwise, quench the fire completely. With your intention, release the fire spirit.

The Role of the Subconscious

THE SUBJECT OF the subconscious is a vast field of study. Since this is a practical handbook, we will focus only on what you need to know about the subconscious in your quest for manifestation skills.

The subconscious believes everything you tell it

This one statement points out very clearly why words are powerful and why becoming conscious of the words you use and think will help you to manifest more easily. For example, if you say or think: "this commute is killing me!" Your subconscious will agree.

Now you have a part of you believing that the commute is killing you. We've already learned that thoughts become things. So, what are you drawing to yourself with these thoughts: a car accident, illness, depression?

HOW TO WORK WITH THE OBSERVABLE PRESENT

If instead you say, "This commute is challenging AND I find something about it to enjoy every day," your subconscious will agree. But now notice you have given the subconscious two thoughts which are not in conflict:

⋄ You have told the truth about the commute being a challenge.
⋄ You have included a wider range of possibilities in that you are finding some things to enjoy.

As a result, you will begin to notice the nice things about your commute: the lambs in the fields, the quality of the light at sunset, the majestic trees at the edge of the highway, the many hawks that peer intently into the field from their vantage points, listening to books on tape, or time for mental reflection.

> Watch your language and your thoughts; they form your reality. Eliminate words from your vocabulary that take your mind down a pathway of negativity. Be vigilant of your every word and your every interaction. You are focusing your subconscious to perceive reality through a different lens.

Notice that you did not lie to the subconscious. You did not say "I love my commute!" The subconscious knows what your current situation is *and* how you feel about it. If you pretend that you love something when you really do not, the subconscious will receive confusing information. It will be forced to choose what it knows to be true: your feelings. However, if you say, "The commute is challenging and I find something about it to enjoy every day," then you have told the truth (the commute is challenging) *and* given the subconscious a new thought (I find something about it to enjoy every day). You have expanded your reality to encompass a larger perspective.

Some ways of thinking are more powerful than others

When athletes compete, they often imagine they possess superhuman powers. They may focus on their legs being longer (runners) or springs on the bottom of their feet (gymnastics). Perhaps they see their fingers are webbed (swimming) or, in team sports, they might think in terms of the individual team members being a flock of birds that act as a unit, turning on a dime and flowing together, sharing a group consciousness.

In our everyday ordinary reality, we know that our feet do not have springs attached and our legs are not longer when we are running, but it serves us if we tell our subconscious to act as if these are true. We are not telling our subconscious to believe this but to act *as if.*

Here is a thought provoking experiment to do with another person: ask the person to stand and extend their arm out from their body at a right angle so their arm is parallel to the floor. Now ask the person to resist you with all their strength as you press down firmly on their wrist. Push steadily until you feel the arm start to give.

Now ask the person to put their arm back into the beginning position. Ask them to imagine an iron rod that is extending from their body all the way through their arm and several feet beyond their hand. Imagine that the rod is unbendable. Have them hold this image in their mind. Now again press on their wrist, using approximately the same force it took to move the arm downward the first time.

What I and thousands of other people have noticed doing this exercise is that it takes much greater force to move the arm when the person is visualizing the iron rod. In some cases, the arm will not budge even when someone is literally hanging on their arm!

> What it does tell us is how we think of things, what we hold in our consciousness, educates our subconscious and has a huge impact on our reality.

There is no physical reason the arm should be harder to move simply because of an intention or visualization. This is where we start to edge over into the idea that we are not simply finite Newtonian beings. We begin to see that our mind has far greater power to affect our physical reality than Newtonian physics predicts.

So how can you use this concept with your stretch goal? Start by visioning yourself accomplishing this goal. Utilize all your different senses to flesh out this vision. Answer these questions: *"When will I complete this goal, where will I be, what will be happening, how will I know it is done, who will be with me, what will I be feeling?"* See the answers in pictures, words or feelings. Allowing a symbol to emerge that captures the essence of your vision is a powerful reminder of your vision.

When I visualized finishing this handbook, I created three scenes to help me crystallize what success looked like.

My first scene was at the printers. I see myself receiving the first copy, turning the first page. I am smiling and in awe. I am touching the cover, noticing its texture.

My second scene is a book signing at a local bookstore. I am signing copies of *The Co-Creation Handbook*, smiling, and handing them back to an enthusiastic audience.

My third scene is travelling to Australia and presenting the handbook in a workshop format to a group of people on November 24th, 2012. I am in front of the group sharing the material. I see the excited faces of the participants. I feel gratitude.

All of these scenes came true. The Australia workshop, the first printing and now the book signing is scheduled.

The symbol that emerged for finishing this handbook was the hummingbird, a persistent, beautiful and acrobatic bird.

EXERCISE: DEVELOPING THE THREE SCENES

Develop three scenes that are all about you completing this stretch goal. Each scene will build in emotional intensity and your final scene will culminate in a triumphant success.

Include: How do you feel, where are you, what are you saying to others and what are you saying to yourself, who is with you, and how are you celebrating?

Write the three scenes down. You will use them with the Audio Program.

Scene One:

_____

_____

_____

_____

_____

_____

Scene Two:

_____

_____

_____

_____

_____

Scene Three:

_____

_____

_____

_____

_____

Action Steps: Week Two

- Every morning and evening for the next seven weeks, start and end your day by listening to the Audio Program. This week use the tracks for Week Two which are "Week Two AM" and "Week Two PM." Make that commitment now. Schedule it into your day and start tonight.

- Journal work: Document your progress towards your stretch goal.

- Each day read the list "Things I Choose to Manifest" from page 47.

- Continue to choose happiness each day.

- Continue to write in your gratitude journal.

- (Optional: perform the Burning Bowl Ceremony.)

WEEK THREE

The Personal Statement

"We were born to paint the truth of our spirit onto the canvas of form,
not to be trapped in someone else's painting."
—Orion Foxwood

Avoiding the Pitfall of the Observable Present

YOU NOW KNOW the most powerful process you can use for manifesting is to tell the truth about your observable present, clarify your vision, notice the creative tension and feel the excited expectancy that arises. Then release and move on with your day. As you move through your day notice what you allow into your awareness. Notice that your observable present is constantly in flux and is changing moment by moment. You are choosing to move forward by consciously creating your vision.

But how do you acknowledge the current situation without focusing on what is going wrong? You do not want to focus on what is not working as that will simply feed energy to those non-working things. And whatever you feed energy to will become more solidly present in your observable present. You may find yourself asking, *"Why isn't this working?"* Remember the subconscious mind. It believes everything. Your subconscious will answer every question, even the ones you did not mean to ask. The subconscious will proceed to tell you *exactly* why this isn't working. Instead, ask a better question. *"How many ways can I find to turn this around AND enjoy the process?"* The word *AND* in this question is very important.

As we search for ways to expand our perception of our here and now, our observable present, we find that the word *AND* helps us. *AND* allows us to hold two things as possibilities. The word *BUT* only gives us a choice of one possibility and the subconscious will pick the possibility it is already familiar with, shutting down the possibility of expansion. When you find yourself using the word BUT, substitute the word AND. Notice the effect this has on you.

The key to telling what you notice about the observable present is to tell it quickly and precisely and then complete the process by moving to the next step of focusing on the vision, noticing the creative tension and feeling the excited expectancy. Cultivate the feeling of excited expectancy; it will irresistibly drive you forward.

This morning Dave arrived for a shamanic training at our home. As he settled in I asked him how he was. He announced, "My back is killing me!" I was concerned that Dave was instructing his subconscious that he was being killed by his back. I asked him if I could make a suggestion to which he agreed. I asked him, "Could you express your pain in a way that speaks the truth about what is going on for you without affirming that it is killing you?" He looked startled for a moment and then a wave of relief washed over his body as he smiled. "Yes, thank you!" he exclaimed. "My back is painful right now AND it is my intention that my back will be pain free!"

Dave stated his back was hurting him right now (the observable present) and then went on to say he was holding the intention that his back would be pain free (vision). Several people immediately stepped up to discuss a method of back care they had found successful. This was a method Dave had not considered before. He left feeling encouraged and excited to pursue a new option.

When you dwell on the drama of the observable present, all you get is increased distress. Sharing again and again all the grisly details serves no one. Speak your observable present once and then move on.

> People often make the mistake of *over* telling their observable present.

When others ask how you are doing, share the process with them. Tell them you are having some challenges but you are working through them. Tell them you are focusing your energy on what you are creating. Share your successes. Put some humor into your stories. Tell them of the synchronicities you are noticing. Encourage them to share their goals, intentions and visions. What would they like to create in their lives? Perhaps they too would like to learn this process and create those things that truly matter to them.

It is important to maintain an anchor in the observable present and it is here that this process is different from an affirmation. Affirmations focus only on the vision and exclude any reference to your observable present. To deny the observable present by focusing only on the vision creates an imbalanced state because you are not grounded in your present moment. You then have no vehicle for any kind of meaningful feedback. No course corrections can be made because you do not know where on the map you are.

You may find, at times, that events happen which are not in alignment with your vision. Those who are not skilled at manifesting will simply give up due to distress.

> At this point the most powerful intervention you can make is to acknowledge the observable present, revisit your vision and ask yourself, *"Do I really want this vision in my life right now?"* If the answer is "YES," formally choose your vision by stating: "I choose _____(insert vision here)" and then—and here is the important part—turn your vision over to the Divine and move on with your day.

You may find at times that the *how's* you have chosen do not lead you towards your vision. When this happens, you must realize that the Flow of Truth is not happening. And then you must search for where the Flow of Truth is in the moment. This moment. For example, if you are piloting a canoe, you want to find where the river current will carry you along. If you come across a still zone, what is the first thing you notice? *That you are not moving.* You then look for another area of the river that is flowing. You avoid chaos in the rapids and pick those parts of the river that carry you along briskly to your destination. Do not be attached to *why* it happens, just move or adjust so you are moving forward. You don't need to know why the river flows to guide your canoe downriver. We will discuss this more in Weeks Four and Five.

So often we become attached to our goals and visions, believing that they *must* be achieved and that the Universe *must* support us. Should your exact vision not manifest, you have a decision to make. Do not stop and ask, "Why is this happening to me?" This is not a useful question for you to be asking. You may never know *why*. Accept the mystery of life and move on to creating. I do encourage you to persist. We know from experience that persistence is a key to successful manifestation. Those who persist against all odds, despite the naysayers, often are successful. Often, goals are forgotten because they do not manifest in the way we think they should or even *when* we think they should. Do not give up prematurely! Once you get a sense of the Flow of Truth you also must consider whether these difficulties are a message from the Universe telling you it is time to move on with a different strategy. If your sense is yes, accept that guidance and do not blame yourself. There is a purpose in it for you. Trust that the Universe is guiding you at all times to something better. When you affirm this wisdom within yourself and make adjustments, you will flow to your destination or somewhere even better.

Let's consider Rita's leaky roof. Rita's stretch goal was to acquire a new roof. For months nothing happened. Every attempt she made to move forward with her stretch goal was met with stiff opposition. She worked her vision from all angles, trying multiple strategies for raising enough capital to fund this project. Finally, on the brink of desperation, she had an inspiration. She returned to the bank and used a different strategy with them. They approved her loan. Then she went out for bid, keeping in mind her vision of what the roof would cost. Two of the bids came in high but the third bid came in just where she had wanted it to, with no compromise on quality.

The Personal Statement

SIR FRANCIS DRAKE, the great explorer, uttered this prayer on a cold day in 1577 … I think it's applicable to you and me, right here, right now.

Disturb us, Lord,
When we are too well pleased with ourselves,
When our dreams have come true because we have dreamed too little,
When we arrived safely
Because we sailed too close to the shore.
Disturb us, Lord, when
With the abundance of things we possess
We have lost our thirst
For the waters of life;
Having fallen in love with life,
We have ceased to dream of eternity
And in our efforts to build a new earth,
We have allowed our vision
Of the new Heaven to dim.
Disturb us, Lord, to dare more boldly,
To venture on wider seas
Where storms will show your mastery;
Where losing sight of land,
We shall find the stars.
We ask You to push back
The horizons of our hopes;
And to push into the future
In strength, courage, hope, and love.

Because you are reading this Co-Creation Handbook, I know you want to make your life bigger, fuller, and more meaningful. I know you want to sail to far away shores, be they metaphorical or literal, finding new horizons you did not even know existed.

There is nothing more dangerous in life than comfort.

The repose of stagnation draws you ever nearer to a precipice where you begin to accept, settle, and acquiesce to the whims of whatever circumstance or paradigm or context the world has trapped you in.

But always remember, my friend, that while society has been cultivated over thousands of years to provide you with limits, to keep order, to ensure that you don't drift too distant from the standard deviation lest you cause a commotion ... you were not made to fit in, you are here to change the world.

—AJ Leon

To create a *life* full of intentional results, you must have a vision for your life. Your vision will give you the direction and definition to manifest what is truly important to you. When asked, those who are expert at manifesting have told us the single most important project they undertook that changed everything else was quite simply recreating themselves as intentional human beings.

Now I introduce you to the Personal Statement. The Personal Statement is your manifesto. It is your statement about who you are becoming, what values you are representing, and what you stand for. By reading aloud the Personal Statement twice per day you are choosing to align yourself with these values. You are beckoning the Universe to align with your intentions. The process of crafting the Personal Statement and reading it aloud twice daily allows you to consciously and intentionally mold your self. You are in charge here. Reading aloud the Personal Statement twice daily will make a lasting change in your physical brain. Your mind will perceive even more of what is already out there and fill in the blanks for what has been missing. You will become the person you choose to be.

In this statement, this manifesto of who you are becoming, you will define what you want to create in your life and what qualities you want to further develop. You will be reading aloud your Personal Statement twice each day. And here is the magic: repeating the Personal Statement with passion causes your body, mind, and spirit to align with your intentions. You will become your Personal Statement. The greater the passion the quicker you will become aligned with your intention.

Already I can feel you starting to get a bit nervous about the Personal Statement. Relax. Personal Statements are meant to be fluid and always evolving as you evolve.

In fact, your biggest job with the first draft of the Personal Statement is to get something on paper. It might feel messy and disjointed at first. That's good; it is authentically *you*. Which brings me to another point: this is *your* statement. You want it to be a reflection of what you want, *not* of what you think you *should* want or what others want for you.

You have to begin somewhere, so begin where you are. If you start taking a stab at something, eventually two things happen: either your aim gets better or you decide that what you are aiming at needs refining. Either way, you win.

Writing the Personal Statement can be a daunting task or an enlightening adventure. You get to choose which it is. Choose adventure. It's so much more fun! And now that we are on this topic, do you want your life to be predictable or an enlightening adventure? There comes a moment in every person's life when they have to consider whether they want to take risks and fully experience life or play it safe and miss out on all the excitement.

Many people will never live fully because they are afraid to step out of their comfort zone. But ironically, if you don't make life an adventure, it is hardly worth living. There is always an inner struggle between the familiar and the unknown.

For example, wouldn't it be great to swim way out into the middle of the lake to take in the amazing view of the mountain's reflection on the water? The view is absolutely incredible out there! On the other hand (gasp!), there are risks involved! What if I have a heart attack or develop a cramp? There will be no one there to rescue me! Fear could hold me back from expanding my experiences.

> I believe each of us can do something every single day to break through some barrier or fear so that life becomes more adventurous, more vibrant, more alive. Do not let life scare you. Be courageous. Let life empower, fascinate, and challenge you! Let life thrill you with its possibilities. Remember, this is the only life you have right now. You don't have another opportunity to relive today. So make it a bold and exciting day. Wring everything out of every moment.
> Do something different, even if it is very small. Something that helps you to feel your aliveness.

These somethings that help you feel your aliveness can be large (climbing a mountain, skydiving, moving to the big city) or small (going on a hike in the wilderness, learning a new skill, turning an acquaintance into a friend, going to a new event). For example: Take another way home. Walk when you would usually drive. Take ten minutes to go to the park and simply sit, enjoying the park with all of your senses. Say hello to a stranger. Learn the name of the person who sells you a cup of coffee. There are millions of things you can do throughout your day to shift your perspective. And barriers are very individual. What may be a small blip for you may be a huge barrier for me. While I encourage you to challenge yourself, I also want you to be gentle with yourself. I say this because I know if you are like most people, you are probably judging yourself to be *less than*. It comes in many flavors: not good enough, never perfect, always behind the crowd.

Are you noticing that you are judging yourself? You have experienced enough of that already in your lifetime. Instead accept yourself as a wonderful being that is starting to open up to exciting possibilities. Take a break from judging yourself. Be aware of your self talk. Don't put up with it any more. Make the choice to talk to yourself in an encouraging, loving way.

If you do find yourself fearful and have the urge to say, "*No, I'm not going to do this, no way!*" try this instead: ask yourself "*how might I enjoy this being possible for me?*" How could I actually *enjoy* swimming out to the middle of that lake? How could I write an audacious Personal Statement? How could I have a more exciting adventurous life? Sometimes, just asking the question will open up your mind to the possibilities of a bigger life.

> Allow your curiosity to be larger than your resistance.

Asking questions in a helpful way will begin to open yourself up to new possibilities. It is the hallmark of a curious mind. And curious minds find areas to explore by digging deeper and considering what most others take for granted. A curious mind is able to look at what other people take for granted and create something new.

One way to broaden your world is to ask your Spirit Helpers to assist you in seeing new horizons to explore. The Audio Program is designed to help you open up to these new horizons. As you ask those open ended questions, you might consider including questions such as: "How can I make my life more of what I choose? How can I grow and expand to live my dreams? What small steps can I take now?"

Ready to write that adventuresome Personal Statement? Trick question: you may never be ready. But it is time.

We will ease into it in stages. So, take the next step . . .

The Current Self

THE FOLLOWING IS a useful exercise because it gives the subconscious plenty to work with. We will not consciously dwell on this once it is written out, but be assured your subconscious will record every pen stroke, every dotted 'i' and every crossed 't.'

In the space below, jot down a description of yourself. You may want to include past accomplishments, your state of health, your living situation and your current relationships. List qualities that you possess and are content with. Are you creative, open-minded, adventurous, passionate, determined, humble, honest, courageous? You may also add in areas that you wish to develop or change.

_____

_____

_____

_____

_____

_____

_____

_____

_____

Writing the Personal Statement

Success comes to those who become success conscious...changing their minds from failure consciousness to success consciousness.

—Napoleon Hill

READ THAT QUOTE again. It embodies the purpose of the Personal Statement.

Applied over time, the Personal Statement will change your subconscious patterns to success consciousness. It will align your subconscious with what you wish to create.

On the next pages you are going to write a description of yourself as you will be in one year. Do not repeat those good qualities that you have already addressed in the Current Self exercise. Only address those qualities you choose to develop. Look through the Current Self description to find areas you would like to shift. For example, if you are underemployed, you might choose to find employment with purpose and meaning. Or, if you have an erratic income, you might wish to create a steady flow of cash which streams consistently into your bank account.

Usually when people write Personal Statements, they sit right down and manhandle it onto the page. While doing this offers some benefits, it usually results in a product that is very much of the linear mind. The mind that got you to where you are today is not the mind you want to help you write your Personal Statement.

For this reason, I am going to ask you to work on this a bit differently. For your preparation, go out into nature or to a nearby park. Take a long leisurely hike or sit on a log under the canopy of trees. Or listen to the flow of the river. Admire the flowers in the nearby field. Listen to the sounds of the natural world. Feel the power of the sun, the cool breeze, the mist. Take your time and let yourself unselfconsciously merge with the rhythms of the natural world. If your access to the outside world is limited, find a small way to engage. Perhaps you can open a window to feel the breeze or admire the small tree planted by the sidewalk on your street, listen to nature sounds on your audio device, or look at a beautiful picture of nature if you cannot go outdoors. Allow your mind to focus on nature and, at the same time, empty your mind of other thoughts.

When we spend time with nature, we replenish ourselves and come home to that part of ourselves that is truly us. Nature provides us the backdrop to separate out what is us and what is other. We are constantly bombarded by what others think of us, want from us. We are, after all, social beings. You may find you have trouble sorting out what you want from what you have been trained to want.

> Taking time in nature will help you to clarify what you want.

If you can, take a notebook with you and, once you've taken some time to relax and enjoy nature, begin working on your Personal Statement.

Here are some guidelines to help you write your Personal Statement:[15]

◇ *Decide which qualities you would like to cultivate from the 5 areas we used in Week Two: Abundance, Work & Projects, Relationships, Appearance, and Health.* Here you can add in the intentions you hold dear for your life. It is not sufficient to say "I want to own my own home." Dwell on why this is important to you; what core value does this desire represent to you? Be definite as to when and in what form. There is a reason for definiteness. Anytime that you set a vision if you have a date associated with it, it galvanizes your consciousness and creates momentum for creating that result.

◇ *Determine exactly what you intend to give in return for what you desire.* What small steps will you take to accomplish this goal? Or are there other offerings you will make not directly related to this? Examples could be tithing, charity work, reducing your carbon footprint on the planet, and good deeds. There is an energy exchange here and the energetic flow needs to be maintained at all times. You need to put out as much or more as you will obtain. To get something for nothing diminishes its value. To help you fully grasp this concept of give and take, I now turn to the Q'ero of Peru, the last living descendants of the ancient Incas and to the word *Ayni* from their native language, Quechua. *Ayni* means mutual help and is used in the culture to express community assistance. For example, when one family is helped by another, at some later time, the helped family will return the effort in some form. The medicine people of the Q'ero speak more clearly of *Ayni* and it is here that we can understand its impact on our abilities to manifest. Q'ero Elder Grandfather Don Humberto Soncco Quispe states that always there must be an energetic flow or there can be no completion. If someone requests help in the form of a ceremony, there must be a very specific exchange worthy of that help or the ceremony simply will not be successful. The Q'ero are so clear on this concept that if the correct *Ayni* is not offered, they will not perform the ceremony since it would be not only an insult to the Spirits but also a waste of everyone's time and effort.

⋄ *Choose a definite date when you intend to manifest what you desire.* I suggest you pick a date six to twelve months from today. Not too distant but with enough time to allow shifts and synchronicities to occur, enough time to allow the Universe to create shifts on your behalf. Begin your statement with the phrase: It is now _____ (fill in the future date you have chosen).

⋄ *Create a definite plan for carrying out your desire, and begin at once, whether you are ready or not, to put this plan into action.* What steps are possible pathways to this goal? What steps are you willing to take?

⋄ *Give thanks to the Divine Being of your preference.*

⋄ *Read your written statement aloud, twice daily, once after listening to the morning Audio Program and once just before beginning the evening Audio Program.* As you read your statement, see, feel and believe yourself already in possession of your heart's desire. Put passion into it! Feel that excited expectation! You may initially feel as though you are faking your enthusiasm. You may feel discouraged. If this happens, ask yourself, "If I could have this, would I choose it?" If the answer is yes, formally choose your statement and persist.

Here is an example of a Personal Statement written by Rhonda W. in October, 2012:

It is now August 2013 and I, Rhonda W., am delighted I am now receiving abundant compensation for my services as a Mentor/Life Coach, Healer, Trainer/Facilitator, Gardener and on site Manager of Cuppacumbalong Gardens and Retreat Centre. I receive over $1500 weekly for my expertise.

I attract and cultivate abundant, fun, win-win loving relationships.

I travel from my home in Australia each year for two months to visit my family and friends in Oregon while stopping off at a new place in the world each year to expand my awareness and heart centre.

I exercise three times a week in addition to strenuous gardening. I eat nourishing foods. I keep my body healthy and fit. I am full of life force energy and glow with the Love of life.

My website[16] is a favorite of thousands with hundreds of hits daily. I write a new blog twice a week full of information about life/plants and gardening, how they relate to emotional challenges and self-help. My courses and CD's are being sold on line with the downloads averaging over twenty per day.

My Bombala house has sold with a smooth transaction at a win-win price. I ask for a new owner to love it and finish fixing it up. I am debt free and building up my savings account each month.

I am happy and at peace with my life, experiencing the knowing that what I am doing is making a positive difference in many people's lives. I am Grateful and Thankful to my God Source, my Helping Spirits and Mentors, for it is done!

Rhonda contacted me just a few days after she had completed writing out her Personal Statement to share the exciting news that her house had sold despite 66 other houses for sale in that tiny town (population 1200) with no new or growing industry. The new owner loves the house and is planning to fix it up, just as Rhonda ordered. This speaks to the power of clarity and persistence. As I consider this house sale from the standpoint of ordinary reality, it was very unlikely to happen. I have visited this house and there was nothing special about it on the surface. So why did this house sell before the other 66 houses for sale? Because Rhonda had the clarity of intention that beckoned the Universe to align with her desires, her intention created a magnetic attraction. In the spirit realms, I can just imagine her house was lit up like a Christmas tree for all to see and be attracted to. And that made this house desirable above all others.

Your Personal Statement

HERE IS SPACE FOR YOU TO WRITE YOUR PERSONAL STATEMENT:

Action Steps: Week Three

- Read your Personal Statement twice per day with passion.

- Continue with the Audio Program using the tracks for Week Three called: "Week Three AM" and "Week Three PM."

- Journal work: Document your progress towards your stretch goal.

- Assess your stretch goal. Is it still right for you? Is it complete? Has it evolved? If so, re-write.

- Continue to choose happiness each day.

- Write in your gratitude journal.

- Read your list of "Things I Choose to Manifest" each day.

WEEK FOUR

Synchronicity

You HAVE NOW been involved with the Co-Creation Process for three full weeks. Write down what changes you have noticed in yourself and in your life:

_____

_____

_____

_____

_____

_____

_____

_____

_____

_____

_____

_____

The Law of Synchronicity

> Synchronicity is the simultaneous occurrence or coincidence of events in life that have special meaning. You may believe that synchronicity arises from a chain of causality or that it comes from a Divine source. You might feel that synchronicities are *God moments*. I do.

IN THE CO-CREATION Process, it is most helpful to think of synchronicity as a direct result of your intentions and as a love letter from the Divine.

Janet puts on her *Observable Present* list that she does not know how to cook. She has the intention that she will learn the art of cooking. Her stretch goal is to learn one recipe each week. The very next day in the newspaper is a review of a new cookbook titled *The "I Don't Know How to Cook" Book*.

First, she may already have been exposed to this book; perhaps she saw it in the bookstore or overheard a restaurant conversation at the next table about the book. But she did not consciously notice because she did not yet have her intention set.

Second, it may be that because Janet clarified her intention to learn to cook, the Universe supplied the answer *and* she was paying attention.

Remember, there are some ways of thinking that are more helpful and more powerful than others. She has many options including investigating the cookbook or simply taking it as a confirmation that her intention is gaining momentum.

Synchronicities are fun in a startling, eye-opening, mind-blowing way. Those God moments remind us we are somehow being noticed by the greater Powers of the Spirit Realms and have a place in the Divine order. I invite you to begin recording the synchronicities happening in your life as you work with the Co-Creation Process.

However you may interpret the source, it is important that you pay attention to synchronicities and be ready to act on them when the Universe serves a ball onto your side of the court.

Remarkably, Earl and his daughter both had the same dream on the same night. The dream was about moving to Albany, Oregon. Here is Earl's experience in his own words:

> *We were living in Carmel, California at the time and we did not even know there was an Albany, Oregon! We looked at each other the next morning and said, "You had the same dream, didn't you?" And we did. We just knew that we both had the dream. I remember we were surprised at the name that came to us was "Albany" since we both thought Albany was in New York. I immediately checked and found out there was indeed an Albany, Oregon. So I contacted the Chamber of Commerce and received their information kit. We found out it was horse country and the kids all had horses, so that was good. And with three kids in private school in Carmel it was costing us $60,000 a year for tuition and we were running out of money. As I looked over the material from the Albany Chamber of Commerce, I read that Corvallis, right next door to Albany, had the number one public school system in the United States, bar none. Great! I thought this is why we had our dream. The kids can continue to have their horses, they will be in a great public school system that won't drain on our finances, and we'll be in Oregon near their favorite aunt.*

Life tells you through synchronicity to do certain things. Life always prevails. When you think you are in control of your creations and your life path, remember you are a Co-Creator. The Divine Universe is the primary creator. When you are proceeding with a goal and you receive synchronistic information that pulls you along in a certain direction or deters you from going in others, check in with how this feels in your body. Is there a Flow of Truth there that is telling you something? It may be an adjustment needs to be made; it may be a big *Go Ahead!* sign; or it may be a major course correction. Ultimately, only you can make this assessment. It is a skill you will develop.

To return to Earl and his daughter's dream, despite the amazing synchronicity, they did *not* move to Oregon at that time. Earl's wife refused to move and the family eventually ended up going broke. Earl divorced his wife. And ultimately, through another series of events, he found himself moving to Oregon. So even though he was unable to respond to the synchronicity of the dream, Life ultimately found a way to get him to Oregon. Even today, Earl believes that if his family moved to Oregon, it would have been so much better for everyone and much less painful than the roundabout way he did take. Now he emphatically says, "When I get a message like that, I don't ignore it!"

The more you begin to listen to the synchronicities, the clearer they become. You start by listening to the big billboard signs of life and then over time you are able to hear the little whispers.

Today as I was sitting at the dining room table, the cover of a book caught my eye. A voice spoke in my mind: "There's something in here for you." Smiling in anticipation, I picked up the book and knowing that I was being directed by the Divine, I opened the book in the middle. I looked down and read the perfect quote for a section of this book I was working on.

And to end this discussion of synchronicity, I have one final question for you:

> If synchronicity is true, isn't it always true?

To answer this in the affirmative with a resounding *yes!* we affirm our understanding that the Universe has endless possibilities and there is an inter-connecting web between all of life. You have everything available to you at any given moment. It is up to you to put together the input you are receiving and play with the energy of the moment. You may not always understand what is coming to you, but it is most helpful to expect that it *is* coming to you now. Look for it! When you are able to adopt this mindset, you increase the likelihood that you will recognize the synchronicities and use them to be in the Flow of Truth. This means whether you are aware of it or not, you are always in a collaborative adventure with the Divine. The Universe speaks in the language of synchronicity. And really, the key is to become aware of it. Creating a clear vision helps you become aware of synchronicities that support the vision.

The Role of Spirituality in Manifestation

> *Our need is the one thing we can give God that God doesn't*
> *already have.*
> —Orion Foxwood

BEFORE WE ENTER into this discussion, I want to address those of you who do not have a spiritual path or a belief in the Divine. Your manifestation results will be just as powerful. In its pure sense, the creation process is neutral. Even those who are agnostic or without spiritual beliefs can benefit by being open to help from a higher power or "mother nature" or the laws of the Universe. Even the shamanic techniques used in the Audio Program are proven methods in and of themselves that do not require a belief in the Divine or adherence to a particular religious belief. While spirituality does provide a sense of depth and meaning to many, we know from our observations of the results of some of the best creators, a spiritual belief system is not necessary for manifesting great results.

For those of you who do have spiritual beliefs, it would be irresponsible of me not to mention the one key element that I and so many of my students have found amplifies our success. I invite you to read over the following and contemplate how you too can invite the Divine to enter into your manifestation adventure, because the Divine is just waiting for your go ahead to unleash the powers of creation.

You Have to Ask

WHEN I REFER to the Divine, my intention is to encompass all those who participate in traditional religions and all those who have an alternative view of Spirit. These methods presented here apply to all those who wish to invite the Holy Ones to partner with them in creating from a sacred place.

Long ago, people believed creativity came, not from their own minds, but from a source outside of themselves, a Divine disembodied muse. Ethnographers have discovered this is also a belief of shamans who journey into non-ordinary realities to meet with magical Divine entities also known as Helping Spirits. In fact, the basis of the word *inspired* is to be inspirited, to be filled with the spirits. In some languages there is no word for imagination because all creative ideas were believed to originate from these Divine assistants. Following this line of thinking, open up to the possibility that any time you have a creative thought, you are being assisted by the Divine.

Your spiritual beliefs will influence who you turn to for Divine intervention and assistance. If you are a religious person, you would pray to the Gods,

Angels, or powers of your faith. For example, you might pray to Jesus if you are Christian or to Kwan Yin if you are Buddhist. If you are a shamanic practitioner, a conjuror, a medicine woman, spirit doctor, magician or healer, you may request assistance from your particular Spirit Helpers. The Helping Spirits from the shaman's cosmology come in countless forms—among them power animals, spiritual teachers, Angels, ascended masters, fairies, elementals, Devas and nature Spirits. There are many expressions of the Divine in our belief systems. Whatever and whoever you believe in or have spiritual experience with can be called upon to help you manifest.

Now back to that statement: *You have to ask*: four little words that will make such a difference in your life if you put them to work.

And how do we, in the great scheme of all there is, get the attention of the Divine and experience those creative juices flowing from us out into the Universe and back again?

Excited expectation.

> When we ask for help, we do so from a stance of Co-Creation. We are not begging or whining about it. We are not victims. What you are is a magical being in human form that can request the door to the seemingly impossible be opened for you and those people and things you care about.

Excited expectation is full of enthusiasm not desperation.

The word abracadabra is a wonderful incantation from the Aramaic. It means: "Let it be so." Many consider that the word "Abracadabra" is actually a Hebrew phrase meaning "I create (A'bra) what (ca) I speak (dab'ra)."

Here is my story of how I discovered how to mesh my ability to manifest with help from the Divine powers, in my case, in the form of Helping Spirits.

When I was thirty seven years old, I had a pattern of being in stable relationships for four years and three months. That's right: I had three relationships that ended *exactly* at four years and three months. I thought this was peculiar. When the pattern repeated again with the ending of my third relationship, I was totally incensed. My anger stemmed from two things.

First, I wanted to find someone with whom I could live out my years and I just could not seem to get through that four years and three months barrier. The second reason was that when I felt my third relationship was failing, I undertook a shamanic journey into non-ordinary reality. Once there, I asked my Spirit Helper if it was time to end the relationship. He assured me it was not and I should persist. Imagine my surprise when my partner terminated the relationship just two weeks later.

I immediately made a journey back to my Helping Spirits. This time I did not ask questions or request guidance. Instead I stated very clearly with a great deal of passion what I wanted to manifest in my life. I gave them every detail I could think of about the qualities I was looking for in a partner: where, when, and why. I was demanding, not exactly polite but not disrespectful. I wasn't going to put up with this bad counsel anymore.

Here is what I asked for: a loving, supportive, fiery man with a great sense of humor. I requested he make an appearance on the scene after six months. I reasoned this would give me enough time to grieve my old relationship and be ready for someone new.

I followed the guideline for generating creative tension and excited expectancy. I began with where I was: I told my Helping Spirits the truth about my observable present including all the intensity of emotion I was feeling. I wasn't sparing them anything, I focused on my intent, seeing, feeling, and knowing success, and then I noticed the creative tension. I felt excited expectation. Then I let go and moved on with my life. I worked on healing my broken heart, figuring out where I was going to live, and stepping back into the role of a single woman.

What I was not prepared for was how quickly the Spirits would respond to my request. Within four months I was developing a friendship with a man. I assumed he was not the one because he had shown up before the six month time frame I requested. But he hung in there and within six months it occurred to me that he was exactly what I was intending to manifest. We have now been together for twenty-one years.

Thank you, Helping Spirits!

And I thank myself for being so focused and passionate and clear about asking for exactly what I wanted.

I have shared this method with many of my students and colleagues. Lorrie B., a Professor of Kinesiology at Western Washington University and a gifted shamanic journeyer, relates her experience with this method:

Alida shared how she had used the Co-Creation Process with her Helping Spirits to call in a relationship. My ears rotated like radar to her comments. I had been out of relationship for a while and had used the usual online matchmaking services to no avail. It was in September when Alida shared with me how I could tell the Spirits directly about my desire to have a special person in my life and that I could make a very firm request. It was apparent that using the channel of the compassionate Spirits to assist this quest was not one I had used in the forlorn longing already experienced in seeking an intimate companion. I journeyed to my Spirit allies and identified wanting someone who was strong, calm and full of compassion and loving kindness.

The day before Christmas, I went to Teddy Bear Cove and did rock grinding[17] for hours. I felt an ancient recognition that the person of my heart was already in my presence.

On Christmas night, a vivid dream came to me: a woman in gold and green gave me the gift of a new Power Animal.

The morning after this dream, I invited Ann to join me and two of my friends for dinner. I assured her that it would be 'no strings attached' since she was still in a long distance relationship. To my amazement, Ann's long distance relationship dissolved almost overnight and we were able to be together.

We move like the strands of our very DNA, weaving close, then separating, then returning. It was through these manifestation teachings that I understood how to stand in co-creative power with my Helping Spirits. With dreams and journeying, I am so content in a relationship that truly is a gift!

Lorrie followed the Co-Creation Process very well. First, she clarified what she wanted. She felt her strong desire in her heart. She had the vision, identified her observable present, and noted the creative tension. She felt that excited expectation. She stepped into her own power and became a conscious Co-Creator with her Helping Spirits. She made several journeys to her Spirit Helpers to tell them very clearly what she wanted. She followed their advice, accepting gifts along the way, and acted on her intuition when she invited Ann out. Synchronistically, Ann's current relationship dissolved and she and Lorrie were free to pursue a romantic relationship.

Remember, you cannot make your vision about another specific person. If you would like to be in relationship, let that be your vision. Do not make your vision 'I want to be in a relationship with a particular person.' You have to let go of the *how* and the *who* and even the *when*.

There are several reasons for this. It is not ethical to try and control or manipulate another for a specific outcome. Nor is it ethical to use your influence to control someone else's fate. You would also be ignoring that the Universe may gift you with someone far more incredible and so much more wonderfully perfect for you than the person you are focusing on. Do not get attached to specific outcomes or people.

Also, be aware that the Universe may throw some solutions at you that are not quite perfect. You might find you have to go back to your vision and remind yourself and your Helping Spirits what it is you really want to manifest.

I am reminded of Carol, a single mother who worked hard to make ends meet and was often very exhausted after a full day of working and single parenting.

A few months ago, I called her. I could hear the excitement in her voice as she shared she had just started a new relationship. We talked about her vision for a relationship and several weeks later, we talked again. The man was not quite working out but, since she was smitten, she was considering compromising on her vision. We reviewed her vision and I asked her if a really great relationship was what she truly wanted. "YES!" she affirmed. And with that, she decided to remain true to her vision and trust that the right person would appear. She said goodbye to the relationship that was not quite right and by closing out that relationship, she made room in her life for something better.

Just a few weeks later she called to tell me that a new someone *did* appear and they were exploring possibilities.

Do not get hung up on the idea that there is only one answer for you. That is just not true. There are *endless* possibilities and many paths to our visions. We need to trust that there is a greater design and if we allow life to flow through us and at the same time, we are an active participant in becoming clear on what we want, affirming what we want with passion, the Universe will present us with the opportunities we need.

At the same time, being an active participant means staying clear on what you want to manifest. It means knowing that when things aren't quite right, it's time to go back and reconnect with your vision and your Helping Spirits. There is a fine balance between trusting what is showing up, staying clear on your vision and not settling for something less than what your soul truly desires.

Soul Purpose and Destiny

> *When you can give up your mental and emotional attachments to what has to be, how it has to be, when it has to be, why it has to be, you open the door to the Holy Spirit. When that energy, the energy of life, light and love enters your world, your life becomes more than you ever dared ask for.*
>
> —Iyanla VanZant

It is GENERALLY assumed that a life purpose is a direct result of the special gifts and talents with which we came into this life. True, there are some individuals who have always known their purpose in life. And then there are those who never know what their purpose is, who spend year after year looking for what they are going to do with a constant sense of feeling lost and forlorn.

Rarely is there only one occupation that can express a soul purpose. Rather, it is our soul purpose that we channel into an occupation. Liz, a dental hygienist, feels her soul purpose is to help others. She has expressed this through many different roles and jobs. As her interests evolve, she may find other ways to express her soul purpose through other types of jobs such as nutritional consulting or health research.

There is a flow you can feel when you are on a path that fulfills your growth and creativity, a path of soul. I call this the Flow of Truth. This is the happy urgency, the excited expectancy, that lets you know when your vision is set and you are leaning hard into it. This is not always the easy path by any means. Ironically, the Flow of Truth is not a "go with the flow" plan. You may find you are going *against* the cultural flow because you have a different vision than the norm. Persistence is often necessary; failures are almost guaranteed. A lot of picking oneself up, brushing oneself off and then stepping forward into a strong headwind is involved. Do not be dismayed or discouraged if your vision is unique. Our world needs diversity to survive and prosper.

How do we discern whether it is our ego talking or our soul talking?

> Your soul knows what it wants – you may need to get very quiet to hear the spirit's guidance. Do you know the difference between when you are praying to God and when it feels that God is praying through you? That is the difference between manifesting from your ego and manifesting from your soul.

We will discuss how to determine what the soul wants next week when we cover the topic called Expanding Outward and Turning Within.

Action Steps: Week Four

- ✧ Continue with the Audio Program using the tracks "Week Four AM" and "Week Four PM."
- ✧ Continue reading your Personal Statement twice per day with passion.
- ✧ Write in your journal for documenting your progress towards your stretch goal.
- ✧ Assess your stretch goal. Time to make it bigger or refine it? Do it! Is it completed? If so, choose a new goal using the same process as before.
- ✧ Each day write in your journal the synchronicities you notice and the things you are grateful for.
- ✧ Celebrate your successes.
- ✧ Decide how you will include the Divine in your visioning process.
- ✧ Read your list of "Things I Choose to Manifest" each day.

WEEK FIVE

Expanding Outward and Turning Within

Help us to be the always hopeful gardeners of the spirit who know that without darkness nothing comes to birth. As without light nothing flowers.

—May Sarton

NATURE TEACHES US that a balance of Expanding Outward and Turning Within is necessary for a system to be healthy. This can also be thought of as expansion and contraction or breathing in and breathing out. Our bodies are linked inextricably to the cycles of nature and we cannot deny the rhythm of ebb and flow. This is seen in the cycles of night and day, the tides, the lunar cycle, the seasons and each inhale and exhale. Winter's rest is necessary for the explosion of life in the spring. This cycle of expansion outward and then turning within is a necessary part of the flow of creation. The health of your very being depends upon your full participation in this cycle of expansion and restoration.

In this modern high tech world, we are doing more than we ever thought possible. Our brains feel full and our schedules *are* full as new demands hit us every day. Think of all the things we now do for ourselves that used to be done for us. We now act as travel agents for our own trips, we act as checkout clerks when we scan our groceries, and we act as bank tellers when we utilize machines to do our banking. We leave voice messages on machines and communicate to our friends with three word texts or, if we are feeling wordy,

Expanding Outward and Turning Within   93

a brief email. We even print our own boarding passes at home so we can go right to the gate without interacting with the ticket counter personnel. We shop on the internet. We even order our prescription drugs online to save money and, as a result, do not receive counseling from the pharmacist at the drugstore counter. When we call a business, we have to figure out which numbers to push to reach a real person. We use a machine to pay for parking at the lot. We search for information online instead of talking to the research librarian. We type our own papers and letters instead of turning them over to an administrative assistant or slowly writing with a pen and paper.

So we have taken on more to do with less social interaction and, as a result, our free time has reduced drastically. We interact with more people than ever but in very truncated, impersonal ways. We were promised a seamless, uncluttered paperless life and have ended up with the opposite. Run, run, run.

We are overloaded with data and possibilities.

Sharon Begley writing for *Newsweek* Magazine in the February 27, 2011 issue discussed research which showed that as information load increases, the area of the brain responsible for decision making, the dorsolateral prefrontal cortex, increases in activity. However, when too much information is received, this area overloads and literally stops functioning. Once this happens, people start making stupid mistakes, frustration and anxiety soars, and their decisions make less and less sense. Too much information is counterproductive to decision making and creates paralysis. Likewise, too much activity is counter-productive to generating new ideas, goals and visions.

Our modern world values expansion at any cost. We are rewarded for producing and constant striving. Even our economic system of capitalism demands constant growth. If the economy is not growing it is considered to be depressed or stagnant. As a product of an expansive culture, on a personal level you may notice that *if nothing is happening, you feel depressed or useless.* This is addiction to stimulation. The urgency to always be doing leaves very little time for rejuvenation, contemplation, and inspiration.

Turning Within

To TURN WITHIN is to create a time of rest, incubation, gestation, contraction and hibernation. In nature we notice that restoration is an essential part of the life cycle. The seasons beautifully demonstrate the concept of Expanding Outward and Turning Within. Autumn is the Turning Within phase, preparing for the dormant state of winter. We notice the days shortening and the crops being harvested. The soil in the garden is put to rest to gather strength for the renewal of spring. In this state, we are resting and regenerating so that once fully restored, we will be able to act on new ideas, concepts, connections, and inspirations received during our regeneration.

There are many levels to Turning Within and you will want to find a level that works for you.

You might choose a way to simply unwind and relax deeply.

The mystics often put themselves into a deprivation experience in order to create spaciousness in their minds and to force themselves out of comfortable but limiting patterns. The idea here is that something is given up in order to create discomfort and to break through old patterns. These patterns limit the way you see the world and what is available to you.

> Breaking these patterns allows you to see the infinite possibilities the Universe has surrounded you with. It is as if you have just eliminated all the static and now can clearly receive the broadcast from the Divine.

You don't have to join a monastery to turn within. Here are several less extreme methods:

- ✧ Turn off the cell phone, put away the computer, throw a cloth over the television screen, and stop answering the phone. Try this for an hour, an evening, or a day.
- ✧ Fast for a day or a meal, minimizing what you are eating or limit food preparation. This will create more spaciousness in your day. We all spend an amazing amount of time involved with eating and a surprising amount of our energy goes towards digesting.
- ✧ Be in silence for all or part of the day. You may go on a retreat where there is no outside stimulus. Just you, resting and restoring.
- ✧ Experience Emptiness. This week, the Audio Program visualization

will take you there.

- ✧ Learn the shamanic journey for power and healing.
- ✧ Move or dance to music or drumming, you can swing your arms wildly or reach up to the sky.
- ✧ Take a warm bath or receive a massage.
- ✧ Experiment with different postures, stances and gaits.
- ✧ Explore your voice with singing and toning.
- ✧ If you commute, switch up your audio habits. Try classical or relaxing music or listen to Ted Talks (www.ted.com) or other inspirational presentations rather than news radio or the top 40.
- ✧ The Audio Program is another way to Turn Within and as you follow the techniques presented, you will be training in the shamanic journey, a time tested way to become a hollow bone. The soothing sound of the repetitive drumbeat will lower your brain frequency to the alpha/ theta states. A bonus is tapping into the wisdom and healing of your Spirit Helpers.

How do you reach that optimal state of creativity? The answer to this is counter-intuitive. The answer is not to do something.

Rather, start by becoming empty. Then state your intention and focus on what you want to manifest. Do this every morning and evening.

How do you become empty?

The first step is to simply acknowledge that your mind is producing thoughts.

The second step is to honor the thoughts that do come. Let the thoughts run their course, the monkey mind chatters for awhile and then it runs down finally to silence (or a dull roar).

The third step: Nothing. That's right. There is nothing to do with the silence. Just let it be there and notice it. Welcome it. As distracting thoughts arise, just acknowledge them, then let them go, and remain quiet.

Like any skill, this takes practice. You will get better at stilling the mind over time.

Creating a receptive space gives your subconscious and the Universe the message that you are ready and available to receive. New and creative thoughts will start to come in. Don't try to generate. This passive state is your opportunity to receive. To be truly co-creative, you must step outside the boundaries of your usual patterns and ways of being. This often requires that you let go of your old ways of thinking and moving. Your mind, so tightly packed with information and minutiae, has to be unpacked. You have to make room for your innovation and genius to arrive. Your body, so used to holding itself in a certain way, can be released to move more freely.

How does Turning Within benefit your efforts to create? In the empty or contracted state, you are much more available for new ideas and directions from spirit to bubble to the surface. Your brain is not full. Pay attention to your urges to rest, sit, and contemplate. Allow your body and mind to rest completely one day or evening a week. Turn off your electronics and your computer one day or evening a week. Allow your mind to rest.

Each day, make some time for you to simply be. Sit and look out the window, enjoy the moment.

The Audio Program is teaching you critical lessons here. If you are not listening to the Audio Program twice per day, make that commitment now and schedule it into your day. Look forward to it, as this process will provide the spaciousness for you to be a co-creative force in your life.

Expanding Outward

All of us, whether or not we are warriors, have a cubic centimeter of chance that pops out in front of our eyes from time to time. The difference between an average man and a warrior is that the warrior is aware of this, and one of his tasks is to be alert, deliberately waiting, so that when his cubic centimeter pops out he has the necessary speed, the prowess, to pick it up.
—Carlos Castaneda

JUST AS IT is important to go within, it is equally important to move outward. In this expansive state, you are moving forward with those new ideas received during the Turning Within state. You are ready and able to engage the world.

Remember, it is a balance of the two states that brings you to the optimal state of creativity. You need both.

If you are Cinderella, you have to get yourself to the ball. She did not sit in her corner, broom in hand, brooding. After she received her inspiration, she got up, got moving, enlisted help, and showed up.

In contrast, Irving decided that he wanted to win the lottery. He thought he could increase his odds of winning if he meditated. After awhile, he decided to improve his chances by meditating in Nature, thinking this would bring him closer to the Divine. Still he did not win the lottery. Finally, he crawled his way up to a high mountain peak where he felt he would be most effective in his meditation. Still he did not win the lottery. In desperation, he called out, "God, why have you not helped me to win the lottery with all that I have done?" The response came swiftly as a voice rang out from the heavens above, "I'd like to help you, Irving, but you have to buy a lottery ticket."

So often when people start to manifest, they spend a few minutes visioning and then give it over to the Universe, plop themselves down on the couch and sit back. They expect the Universe is going to supply everything and deposit whatever is desired at their doorstep, wrapped up with a bow.

This is a misunderstanding of the Co-Creation Process. This misunderstanding is a common reason people fail at creating.

To be a Co-Creator is to be an *active* participant in creating your life. As you co-create, you become involved in a game of sorts:

> *Imagine a tennis court: you on one side, the Universe on another. You open with a serve and land the ball on the other side. The Universe receives it and lobs it back to you. Now the ball is slightly changed in trajectory and speed. You have to hit it again with a different force. You hit it back. You are playing. So is the Universe.*

What this example tells us is you cannot hit one serve and expect to win the tournament. After you hit the ball, look for what is coming back to you. Once you set your goal and run through the observable present/vision/creative tension/excited expectancy format, you have sent that ball out into the Universe. Now anticipate that the Universe is giving back. Be eager to hit the ball again.

Maybe it is your Aunt Cora calling to invite you to the Garden Club meeting on dahlias. You think, gosh no, no interest in dahlias. Oh but wait, there may be an opportunity here for the Universe to make a connection

for you: if you go, you will meet someone who connects to your passion of
_____(Fill in the blank).

Open up to all the creative and magical ways the Universe is answering your call. Be confident. Go to the dahlia meeting expecting that there will be a clue there for you to help progress towards your vision or the right person to help you to the next step.

Yes, that's right. You have to get out there and mix it up. Tell everyone what you are looking for. People love to help and they have resources and connections you have not even dreamed of. Keep moving. Keep asking. Doors will open.

Sometimes the response from the Universe is immediate. You get a call or bump into just the right person to help you move toward your goal. Other times it seems like the Universe forgot all about you.

> The Universe does not forget you.

Realize that sometimes many things have to fall into place to create what you are intending. There may be a time delay. Time delay is often an important aspect of co-creating. You may think nothing is happening but you do not know all that is happening on your behalf somewhere else. What amazing series of events are being lined up just for you? This can take time. This is why persistence is one of the most important characteristics of successful people. You have to be involved long enough for the ball to land back in your court in a way that you recognize it so you can then return the serve.

And what if sometimes those first steps look downright scary, even though you have a sense that is what you should be doing? Go ahead and take the risk. Be brave! Now is better than later—which is so much better than never.

What do you do when movement is stalled completely on your goal? Let's go back to Rita's stretch goal of a new roof for her home. The house was desperately in need of a new roof and if one was not installed by the fall rains, she would need to put a tarp over her roof to prevent the leaks from entering the house. She followed the prescribed course and faithfully listened to the Audio Program, read her Personal Statement, and did the exercises. She was on track.

But nothing was happening. After seven weeks, she was frustrated. And she could not figure out how to create movement with this goal beyond the steps she had already taken.

In our discussions, I realized that Rita's stretch goal generated distress, tapping into her issues about money. The more she worked with the stretch goal, the greater her frustration, opening the doorway for negative self-talk. Remember, the stretch goal is a goal which helps you to train the subconscious and works best when it does not tap into deeper issues.

To resolve this, we reviewed her *Things I Choose to Manifest* list for other goals that did not tap into deeper issues. We decided to switch her stretch goal. Her new stretch goal had many possibilities for forward movement and did not cause her emotional distress.

The next day she wrote to say she was well on her way to creating the workshops to help her share her gifts (her new stretch goal). And the workshops would generate income for her. Her movement with this goal has caused other goals to leap forward as well. And as she generates income, she is closer to paying for her new roof.

Refocusing on a different stretch goal allowed Rita to relax and enjoy the process which in turn spilled to other areas of her life. In her newly relaxed state, she received inspiration to try a different tactic and this time, she received the necessary funding for her roof.

This is a critical lesson for all of us: when one area is not flowing, focus on another area and soon everything will begin to flow. This is not giving up. The original goal is still in the background ready to move to the front.

Don't beat yourself up because one goal seems stuck.

Do move your focus to goals that are rich with movement opportunities. But do not give up on the "stuck" goal. Keep the "stuck" goal on your list of *Things I Choose to Manifest*.

Watch what happens.

Another answer to the question "What do I do if nothing is happening with my goal?" is to open up to your intuition by paying attention to the little voices in your head. Those little voices or thoughts that remind you what to do and bring creative possibilities to your attention are the Divine Beings talking to you. If you pay attention to the small voices and act upon them, you will encourage them to keep talking with you and sending you information and ideas. The intuitions will become more prominent and refined over time. If you treat these thoughts as if they have a deeper intelligence, you will reinforce that they do indeed have a deeper intelligence. They will then surprise you with their wisdom and guidance. If you have trouble acknowledging that these seemingly random thoughts in your head could be the voices of the Divine talking directly to you, remember in Week Two we discussed how some ways of thinking are more powerful than others. If you allow yourself the possibility, if you act *as if,* you are expanding out of your observable present. You are engaging that part of your brain that enables you to create seemingly miraculous results or at least results better than you were getting before.

> Remember that this is a co-creative venture in partnership with the Divine. You are an important partner in this work and you must call upon your discernment. At no time should you blindly follow any guidance without tempering this advice with good common sense.

I remember a client who came to see me who had recently lost all her money. A few years earlier she had begun channeling a spirit who encouraged her to spend all her money, even her retirement funds. She followed this advice without thinking of the consequences. She did not partner with this spirit in a co-creative venture; instead she handed over all the decisions to this spirit just as a child would to a parent.

Treat these voices like an experiment. Follow their advice if possible; measure the results. If the results are neutral to positive, continue to work with them.

Keep Going

When you're traveling, ask the traveler for advice, not someone whose lameness keeps him in one place.

—Rumi

Some of you have the tendency to stop. This section is for you and is about how to keep going.

Newton's First Law of Motion states that a body at rest tends to stay at rest and a body in motion tends to stay in motion. It is harder to make a course correction on a body at rest than it is to correct a body in motion.

> **Momentum** is a commonly used term in sports. A team that has momentum is on the move and is going to take some effort to stop. A team that has a lot of momentum is really on the move and is going to be hard to stop.

In terms of Co-Creation, this means you need to be out there engaged. Start to do something toward your goal—anything. Once you start to see things are happening, encourage it, shape it, and work with it. Even though you are engaged in activity and movement toward your goal, at the same time you are still not attached to the specifics of how your goal will be met. Perhaps something will come along that will take you just part way there, as in this story:

> *A young man is hitchhiking to Miami from Alaska. He has been on the side of the road for a long time, so long he is very cold and can barely hold up his sign. After many hours, a friendly trucker stops. He says, "I'm not going to Miami but I can take you as far as Fort Lauderdale." Dejectedly, the young man turns the ride down.*[18]

You can see how holding on to a specific pathway for getting to our goals does not always serve us. Sometimes the Divine offers other solutions and, to keep moving, we hopscotch our way to the finish line. Nothing wrong with that!

For example: if your goal is to run a 10k race but right now you can only run a half block, the First Law of Motion says to put yourself into action and to continue those actions that move you closer to your goal. Some of the ways you might do this are

- ✧ run the half block
- ✧ run the half block two or three times a day
- ✧ run the half block as fast as you can
- ✧ when ready, run a full block
- ✧ watch the movies and read the magazines and books devoted to this subject
- ✧ tell everyone you are training for the 10k and now can run a full block
- ✧ go to the running store and talk to the clerks about running (they are experts)
- ✧ go to the running club meetings
- ✧ tell your friends your goal; ask for their input
- ✧ tell your neighbors and other acquaintances; ask for their input
- ✧ go to a 10k race and volunteer to help
- ✧ develop three scenes that are about you running a 10k race

And once you sense that you are making progress, do more of that. If the running club meetings are motivational and you are meeting running partners there that get you out running, do more of those meetings. Do anything that verifies to your subconscious: "Yes, indeed, this is possible!"

Love it, breathe it, do it. The options for creating momentum toward your goal are endless. If you come up empty and cannot think of options for moving forward, you may need to ask for help because you are blocking your options even if you don't think you are.

Often, in order to keep our momentum going, we realize we need to ask for help. We run into an obstacle that we just do not know how to deal with. When we ask for help, we can sometimes feel very small. The very act of asking reminds us of all the times we were powerless as little children. Remember, your creation is not just about you. It is about what you are creating. A skilled creator will use all possible resources to bring his or her creation into being.

Carry this lesson over into all areas of your life. If you feel stuck, ask yourself or others: What do I need to investigate? What question am I not asking? Is there a resource I need to tap into? Do I need to look at this challenge in a different light? How can I do that? Be curious.

How can you generate momentum when you don't feel like getting off the couch? Sue W. encounters this question all the time when she exercises. Her mindset does not naturally go to "let's exercise!" It goes more towards, "Let's stay in bed, let's eat, let's be comfortable." The way she met this resistance to her exercise goal was by first acknowledging that she did not want to exercise (she told the truth about what she observed to be true in the moment). Then she negotiated with herself. "OK, self, I will just put on my running clothes." Once she had her running clothes on, she felt like running. She wanted to move. It was so easy to step out the door and start! And on those days when she still did not want to run, she walked outdoors, looked up at the sky and began to move her body. She walked. She experimented with how it felt to jog. And then she transitioned into a run.

So begin by doing the foundational work. If your goal is to write, then clear off your desk, open your computer up, sit down, and review what you have done. Start with one small effort and soon the momentum will build and will move you along.

The Helping Spirits are very willing to help you with blocks. During the Audio Sessions, consider asking your Spirit Helper the question, "What is one small thing I can do to create movement with this goal?"

Action Steps: Week Five

- Continue with the Audio Program Week Five, "Week Five AM" and "Week Five PM."

- Continue reading your Personal Statement twice per day with passion.

- Assess your stretch goal. Is it still right for you? Is it complete? Has it evolved? If so, re-write.

- Journal work: document your progress towards your stretch goal.

- Journal work: record your successes with Turning Within and Expanding Outward.

- Journal work: write down those things you are grateful for.

- Read your list of "Things I Choose to Manifest" each day.

WEEK SIX

Boundaries

"It is only with boundaries and limitations that we can create anything. Once created, those boundaries can be pushed. This is the nature of evolution. This applies to everything—art, poetry, life, relationship, love."

—Kristi Stout

WHO OR WHAT have you chosen to surround yourself with? We are not islands. We are influenced by our environment. Use this fact to your advantage. Consciously choose to surround yourself with those things and people that move you towards your desired results and intentions.

First, assess what in your environment helps you to maintain an inner sense of happiness and optimism. And second, identify who or what in your life inspires you to move forward.

Let's begin by looking in the three areas of media, relationships and personal space.

Media

MEDIA HAS A profound effect on our conscious, subconscious and unconscious states. Media surrounds us and begs for our attention everywhere we go. Today it takes a conscious effort to screen out media and be in silence. Media can be a powerful tool for your growth but you must be aware of how it impacts you. You may not be able to always control your exposure to media but you can become more aware and make conscious choices regarding how media impacts your decisions, your emotions, and your goals.

One form of mass media, music, has profound and pervasive effects on our emotions. Be very conscious of what type of music you surround yourself with – is it uplifting or depressing, is it positive or negative wording, does it sedate you or help you come alive with enthusiasm? Music penetrates right past our consciousness and into our subconscious. Even if we do not understand the lyrics consciously, our subconscious records it all.

The different genres of music have been studied and the conclusion is different types of music elicit different emotional responses and because of this, we can conclude when a person listens to music they are essentially handing over their emotional state to what is being played. Rap music tends to elicit aggression. Classical music tends to reduce crime, increase spending and be calming. Many surgeons use classical music to relax their patients before surgery. The intensity of rock music elicits many feelings: happy, sad, mad, annoyed, or pumped up. This intensity can lead to an emotional release leaving the listener feeling happy and relaxed. Country music often dwells on heartache. While fans may sometimes feel dragged down emotionally, other fans find that the lyrics reassure them that they are in good company.

Loyalty to a genre that elicits intense feelings of sadness and anger can be problematic for those who wish to consciously co-create. If you want to manifest happiness, successful relationships, fulfilling job situations, abundance, and health, ask yourself if the music you are listening to is supporting those qualities in you.

Choose your music carefully. We know that happiness facilitates manifestation. Therefore, consciously seek out music that elevates your mood and encourages you to activate your potential. If you feel as if you are losing touch with your inspiration, go back to the shamanic drumming track in the Audio Program. Simply listening to the steady beat of shamanic drumming has been proven to elevate the mood, reduce pain, and sharpen mental functioning.

Television is another boundary area to pay close attention to. Make choices about what you watch and what emotions are generated as you watch. What is presented as "The News" is skewed to sensationalism and fear and includes only those stories that a few organizations want you to view. The news stations are now mostly controlled by two or three companies with vested interests in influencing your thinking. They want you to believe what will benefit them. As a result, the news and many TV shows are focused on creating fear and upset. The more time your brain stays in a state of fear and upset, the harder it is to be open-minded and get your brain into a creative state.

Twenty three years ago when I was trying to leave my safe corporate job and risk being self-employed, I heard a wonderful lecture given by a woman who channeled a spirit named Bartholomew. What she said was so profound, it made a huge change in how I perceived my emotional reaction of fear. She said, "Where there is fear, there can be no love. Where there is love there can be no fear." I realized that every time I am in a fear state, I cannot open my heart to fully embrace all the possibilities that are available to me. I went back to this phrase many times as I readjusted to my new lifestyle and it helped me jump the hurdles of fear as I released the familiar and opened to new opportunities.

The advertising and shows on television and in other forms of media are geared to increase your desire to spend money on things you do not need. If you are an average TV watcher, you have watched thousands of television commercials each year. Each commercial is developed by a team of highly skilled professionals determined to appeal to your subconscious emotions and focus you, their captive audience, on what they want you to buy, not what you want to create. And if you are pleased to own a device that allows you to fast forward through commercials, they have figured out a way to reach you. The marketers now place advertising within your television show so you cannot avoid it.

Each time you make a choice to watch television, remember you are volunteering to spend your precious time watching someone else's story and opinion about who you should be and what you should want rather than creating your life.

Social media has some of the same concerns. You are not living your life if you are constantly reviewing others' lives. Use social media conscientiously and sparingly. Use it only to connect meaningfully with your friends and network with other professionals. Decide how much time you choose to devote to social media and set a timer each time you engage with it.

Relationships

THE PEOPLE YOU surround yourself with can be your most important allies or your biggest stumbling blocks. Choose them carefully. Choose people you admire and want to emulate. Choose those who stretch you to become more than you are today, who ask you thought provoking questions, who vibrate with happiness, who challenge you, who lift you up, who make you laugh. Choose relationships that welcome new people and look to build on the best in everyone. Find those people that make you curious about how they manifest. Choose those people for your friends. Spend your valuable time with people that add to your growth.

It may be time to have a heart to heart talk with some old friends if you find the two of you are talking about other people instead of ideas or you are dragged down by their gossip or negativity. Do not let them steal your opportunity to move forward in life by depleting your energy. You may choose to limit your interaction with them. Or you might invite them to learn the Co-Creation Process. You may inspire them by being the role model they need to change their way of interacting with the world. Ask them to join you on this journey and share with them the Co-Creation skills you are learning. See how they respond to your invitation to become the Predominant Creative Force in their own life. They may jump at the chance. And if you have to say goodbye, do so with love. Do not end this relationship by modeling the very behavior you wish to say goodbye to.

Perhaps you have family members that sabotage your efforts to become the Predominant Creative Force in your life. We know that family is precious; when everyone else deserts us, it is family who sticks by us. We do not want to cut away part of our family. We want our family to support us, lift us up, and help us to reach our dreams. With this in mind, begin to bring this issue into your intention. You could word it this way: I am able to relate to _____ in such a way that my creative processes are enhanced. Or choose a wording that is more relevant to your situation.

As you change, expect that your relationships will change too. For example, if you choose to be a non-smoker, those friends you are habitually socializing with on the break at work may not be the best choices if they are smoking. Meet them at a non-smoking venue.

The person that you spend the most time with is the one who most influences your frame of mind and your ability to create. Who is the person you are most in contact with? Why, that would be *you*.

Watch your self talk. What do you tell yourself? What questions do you ask yourself? Are you comparing yourself to others and asking "Why can't I do that?" Your subconscious is a powerful machine. If you ask yourself, "Why can't I do that?" it will start showing you exactly why you can't. And that reinforces the belief that you can't.

Better instead to engage the subconscious with carefully worded questions such as: "What is my vision for this?" or specifically "What is my vision for fulfilling work?" "Who is an inspiring person to have dinner with?" "In what ways can I enjoy doing this and be wildly successful at it?" Now you have the subconscious working on your side.

You know for a fact that thoughts influence actions so take control of your thoughts and encourage yourself. You are the captain of your ship and the master of your fate. If you don't believe it, no one else will.

To support yourself when the self confidence is waning, fill out an Atta Girl/AttaBoy sheet. This is a piece of paper upon which you write the good things about yourself and the good things you have done. The purpose of the Atta Girl/AttaBoy sheet is to encourage and inspire you by reminding yourself of who you truly are and what you have accomplished. Read it daily this next week. And especially pull it out when you are noticing negative self talk. We have been trained to forget ourselves, to forget what is good and true about ourselves. It is time to remember. Make a note on your calendar to pull your sheet out monthly to update and review.

A final suggestion on relationships is to find a Co-Creation buddy for accountability. This is a person that you check in with perhaps twice a week that holds you accountable to your dreams, who reminds you of your greatness. In return, you will hold your buddy accountable and encourage them to move towards their visions.

AttaGirl/AttaBoy

List good things about yourself and good things you have done.

_____

_____

_____

_____

_____

_____

_____

CO-CREATION BUDDIES REVIEW A CHECKLIST WITH YOU:

◇   Are you working with your stretch goal?

◇   Are you using the Audio Program morning and night?

◇   Are you reading over your list of intentions and your Personal Statement?

◇   Are you staying detached from the 'how' and staying focused on the results?

◇   Are you recognizing the synchronicities as they happen and staying flexible?

◇   In what ways are you integrating Expanding Outward and Turning Within into your life?

◇   Are you reading over your Atta Girl/AttaBoy sheet? Are you remembering what is good and true about yourself?

Personal Space

You may believe that what happens in your personal physical space has no effect on how you manifest your dreams. There is an entire profession that disagrees with you. They have backed their belief with concrete examples of how their clients' lives changed when they cleared out the clutter. Yet clutter has reached an epidemic in the United States. Here are some statistics from the National Association of Professional Organizers:

- The U.S. Department of Energy reports that one-quarter of people with two-car garages have so much stuff in there that they can't park a single car.
- Cleaning professionals say that getting rid of excess clutter would eliminate forty percent of the housework in an average home.
- We spend one year of our lives looking for lost items.
- Twenty three percent of adults say they pay bills late (and incur fees) because they lose the bills.
- If you rent a storage facility to store your excess belongings, you're contributing to a $154 billion industry – bigger than the Hollywood film business.
- 1 in 11 US households rents a self-storage space spending over $1000 a year in rent.
- It costs an average of $10/square foot/year to store items in your home.
- 27 percent of consumers nationwide said they feel disorganized at work, and of those, 91 percent said they would be more effective and efficient if their workspace was better organized. 28 percent said they would save over an hour per day and 27 percent said they would save 31 to 60 minutes each day.
- Stephanie Winston, author of The Organized Executive,[19] estimates a manager loses one hour/day to disorder, costing the business up to $4,000/yr if earning $35,000/yr – or $8,125/yr at $65,000– or $16,250/yr at $130,000.

Clearing clutter creates space in your life for new insights, energy, joy, and experiences to come in. Just as we de-clutter our mind in meditation, we free up our ability to create by freeing up space in our dwellings. Remember: as without, so within.

One de-cluttering axiom which I find helpful:

Do you love it or use it?

If not…out it goes.

De-cluttering can be a great stretch goal because quick results assist us in re-educating our subconscious about what is possible. One TV show, Clean Sweep, brought this point home to me very elegantly. On the show, host Peter Walsh was giving tips on de-cluttering. One tip was the stuff of genius. Take one kitchen drawer, pull it out, set in on the counter, and work on de-cluttering the drawer for ten minutes (set your timer). Completing this small task gives the subconscious the clear message that you are successful at eliminating clutter and also successful at completing a task.

My colleague, Jo F. of Bozeman, Montana, is a talented songwriter and shamanic healer. She had one entire room of her house devoted to junk. She used the manifestation techniques to clear out the room and today enjoys a spare bedroom in her home. Jo describes her process: *"I went into the room and saw it without the clutter. I gave myself a year. I SAW it in one year, totally clear of all that was in it. I don't even remember taking the stuff out. It just happened bit by bit and a year later the room was clear."* This is a wonderful example of how the subconscious responds to clear mental direction. Jo did not put a big effort into this process: she simply acknowledged her observable present, clearly envisioned and anticipated her result, and then let go of the hows.

Work/Life Balance

WHILE YOU WANT to be successful in your profession, burnout does not mean success. And your boss's goals may not be your goals. To maintain a work/life balance, you might do the following:

- Commit to one day completely off work a week.
- Limit after hours work emails.
- Commit to a date or friend night with the work phone and email off.
- When not on call do not put yourself on call.
- Balance work goals with social and personal goals.
- Make vacation a complete break from work. No phone calls. No emails. No texts. No contact. If work colleagues tend to violate your vacation boundaries, tell them you will be out of communication range during your time off. ("I'm going backpacking and will not have internet access.")

Action Steps: Week Six

- Assess your stretch goal. Is it still right for you? Is it complete? Has it evolved? If so, you may choose a new stretch goal or refine it.

- Continue with the Audio Program Week Six using the tracks "Week Six AM" and "Week Six PM."

- Continue reading your Personal Statement twice per day with passion.

- Assess what and who you surround yourself with. Decide on any steps to take to support your ability to become the Predominant Creative Force in your life.

- As you notice self talk that does not support your Co-Creation Process, write down the self talk. Reframe this self talk to engage your subconscious to help you create what you want. Example: "I'll never be able to give up sugar." Rewritten: "I am curious about how I will give up sugar."

- Become aware of mind clutter. Set a timer for five minutes. When the timer goes off, write down what you have been thinking about for the last five minutes.

- Write your Atta Girl/AttaBoy sheet. Read it each morning this week after listening to the Audio Program.

- Read your list of "Things I Choose to Manifest" each day.

WEEK SEVEN

Opening Up Your Perception

"The Universe is full of magical things patiently waiting for our wits
to grow sharper."
—Eden Phillpotts

You've been working with the Co-Creation Process for six weeks now and you've noticed significant movement with some, if not all, of your goals. However, you are probably also suspecting that you are missing some obvious opportunities that could have moved everything along quicker. Noticing of missed opportunities, in itself, is an opportunity of major significance.

As I look back on what I have created, I often wonder how I could have
created it quicker, how could I have immediately made those connections
to groups that would have opened up all kinds of doors, and how could
I recognize which paths to run down when they first appeared.

Have you also had these experiences?

I bet you have. Looking at things in retrospect always gives us the perspective of how we can do it differently the next time.

There is only one problem with that line of thinking: the creative person often creates something once and then moves on to the next vision.

So the question now becomes *"how can you easily open up to the best possibilities and tap into your resources even more quickly so you won't miss those golden opportunities?"*

The answer is found in how we habitually perceive reality and in how we use our emotions to filter our observable present. We all have our own unique ways of absorbing input. Some of us see a huge picture, some of us are more sensitive to certain kinds of opportunities, and some of us notice only what is right in front of our nose.

We also know that emotions affect our electromagnetic signature. We are all interconnected at a deep level through our electromagnetic fields. We are truly all One.

The Integral Theory of Everything[20] proposes that there is a cosmic field present throughout nature that stores information about our world. The field is continuous and carries information as well as energy. This information and energy storing device is called the Akashic field. Akashic means all pervasive and fundamental, the basis of all.

This Akashic field informs all living things, the entire web of life, and even our own consciousness. You do not need to go to the Sphinx in Egypt or anywhere special to tap into the Akashic Field. It is available to you right here, right now.

As we intuitively absorb information from this field, we subconsciously screen out what is not in our accepted world view. Like Archie Bunker, the opinionated patriarch of *All in the Family*, the American sitcom originally broadcast in the 1970's, we reject new ideas that stretch our comfort zones and gravitate instead to those viewpoints that reinforce the beliefs we already hold.

So how can we more clearly, completely and quickly perceive the observable present?

As I pondered this question, the Universe showed me a fabulous way to conceptualize this with a term from, of all places, ophthalmology.

Scotomas

SCOTOMAS ARE A self-imposed contraction of perception, an inability to perceive something. We can have a clearer, more expansive view of our observable present, our here and now, by ferreting out scotomas.

A scotoma is an area of partial alteration in the field of vision consisting of a partially diminished or entirely degenerated visual acuity that is surrounded by a field of normal – or relatively well-preserved – vision.

While scotoma is specifically a term used in ophthalmology, for our purposes, we can broaden the definition of scotoma to include blind spots of another kind, namely, the blind spots we have in our observable present. This concept of scotomas can be very useful to us as we look at ways to expand our consciousness in our everyday lives. Once we are aware of a blind spot or scotoma, then we can see it for the self-imposed limitation it is and identify ways to move through it.

How many times have you looked for something that you knew was right in front of you but you could not see it? That is a scotoma.

Now think about all the times you had a problem and you knew the answer was very close but you just could not find it. That is a scotoma.

The problem with scotomas is this: sometimes you don't even know they are there. However, when you suspect their presence, you are on your way to finding the solution. This is how the human brain works. The brain perceives what it is used to perceiving. Our perception is not comprehensive so our brain fills in the gaps. And when gap filling, our mind uses what is familiar and not always correct.

Often the first step in recognizing the scotoma is to ask a question whose answer requires "out of the box" thinking. Sometimes you need to be shaken up and threatened with loss before you will question how you could do things differently. Sometimes, the motivation needs to be heightened to a crisis level.

In 1949 a forest fire broke out in Mann Gulch, Montana. Smoke jumpers were parachuted in a team of fifteen headed by a foreman named Wag Dodge. The fire exploded. It was moving over six hundred feet per minute—faster than most people can ever run—and so fifteen firefighters were trapped. Wag Dodge had an idea. He knew they would lose the race back to the top of the ridge, so he suddenly stopped and lit a match. He lit a fire at his own feet. And the fire spread around him. I imagine the other smokejumpers thought the guy was crazy. But his idea was this: if I burn the fuel around me, then when the fire comes and overtakes me, I am safe. I'll be in what came to be known as an escape fire. He tried to get the other smokejumpers to join him and nobody did. The fire overtook the crew killing thirteen men and burning thirteen hundred acres. Wag Dodge survived nearly unharmed in his escape fire. It is just tragic to think of the answer being there but in the moment not being able to see it. That's how embedded people get in the status quo—they can't recognize an invention when it's among them and they can't give up their old habits.

—Dr. Don Berwick, Head of Medicare/Medicaid from 2000-2011

Here we have a desperate situation and a man, Wag Dodge, capable of creative thinking under stress. Unfortunately the other smokejumpers were unable to process Wag's new idea logically for two reasons: they had a scotoma which prohibited them from recognizing the solution to their problem and their fear of fire at their feet stopped their brains from processing and accepting the new possibility. As a result, they made the irrational decision to run for it, even though they knew the fire would overtake them.

I first encountered the concept of the scotoma in a management training course in creative problem solving. I thought the scotoma concept was an interesting idea, but not relevant to me because I was an open-minded, aware person. (Hint: if you think you don't have scotomas, you do.) But something shocking happened two days later that changed my perception of reality.

I was browsing through Roger Tory Peterson's *Field Guide to Eastern Birds*. I came across a picture of an unusual looking bird, the yellow headed blackbird. As I read the description and examined the picture, I said to myself there was no way that bird could be found in my area. Because this bird was so flamboyant, I assumed I would certainly have seen it by now. Just as its name implies, it is a large blackbird with a brilliant yellow head. I, being an observant person, could not have missed it. (Of course, confidence that you could not have missed something is a clue that there may be a scotoma involved.) Much to my surprise, the guidebook stated that the bird was found in my area.

Remembering my introduction to scotomas, I decided to put the theory to the test. I had already acknowledged that a guidebook I trusted stated that the bird did exist and was an inhabitant of my area. So my brain was now open to seeing the bird. I consciously made a choice that I would see this bird. I did not put a timeline on it but I did have a sense of happy urgency about it since I enjoy birds and wanted to see this one.

The very next day, I was looking out my picture window when I noticed an unusual bird. I looked closer and saw a small blackbird but it had a yellowish tinge to the feathers on the head and neck. I pondered for a second what this bird could be. It certainly did not have the striking pure yellow head I had seen pictured in the guidebook. Then I wondered, could this be the female yellow headed blackbird? Females often have more subdued plumage than the males.

I ran to the book and looked up the female's picture and yes, it was the female. Wow! Where is the male? I looked again curious to see if the male was close by and, right on cue, the male yellow headed blackbird strutted into view. My jaw fell open in disbelief! I had just very clearly uncovered my first known scotoma. I knew that this bird had been around all the time. But because I was unaware of its existence, I did not look for it and therefore I did not see it. After my first sighting, I saw these birds frequently.

At that moment I had the revelation that what I saw and *experienced* in my reality was very dependent on what I *expected* to see and experience. I began to understand that I was indeed a Co-Creator of my world and, unfortunately, not always in a positive sense. I was an active participant in creating a world full of limitations. And, as Richard Bach so eloquently stated, "Argue for your limitations, and sure enough, they are yours!"

I could not help but admit I had limited my own perception of reality. The yellow headed blackbird became a symbol for me of increased freedom. I now could give myself the challenge of finding new ways to be, see, hear, taste, to expand beyond my small perceptual "backyard." I knew there were things I had accepted as absolute truth that were not. I was off on a grand adventure to find them. And for me it all started with a bird.

One way to work with the scotoma concept is to acknowledge that everything you want to create is already available to you in the Akashic field. You just need to take off the blinders so you can recognize it, put your attention on it and allow it to become part of your world.

How do you take off those problematic blinders?

Use the Co-Creation Process: identify what you want to create, hold that vision, acknowledge your observable present, notice the creative tension and feel the excited expectancy that you will be able to break through any self-imposed perceptual barriers. Then pay attention to what comes into your field. Affirm to yourself that unexpected ways to create will appear. In other words, treat this just as you would a new goal: be clear on what you want, be truthful about your current reality, feel the excited expectancy and then move on with your day.

Other scotoma examples:

- Claire read an article about beekeeping and developed a curiosity in learning more. Within a few days she noticed the sign at the corner of her block announcing *An Introduction to Beekeeping* at the local Grange.

- Sophie's home was in need of a new front door and she wanted operable side windows on the door to improve the ventilation in her home. The door shop said they did not offer side windows that opened. That just seemed wrong to Sophie. She could see the door with operable side windows clearly in her mind. As she looked through their catalog, she found exactly what she was looking for and the door shop sheepishly agreed to order it. The door shop personnel had the scotoma. They were so sure the option did not exist they could not even see it in their own catalog.

- As I drive into the grocery store parking lot, I get the feeling that I will not find a close in parking spot and I will have to walk from the far lot today. Despite this, I go through the mental gymnastics of trusting my parking lot genie to manifest a spot by the door. I enter the lot and stop, looking around. No, there doesn't seem to be one here. I linger as I consider that I asked my genie for a spot so there should be one here and perhaps the problem is my attitude. So I mentally change my expectation from expecting failure to one of expecting the spot to be there. Then with a jolt I notice the empty parking spot right in front of my car. Literally, it could not have been closer. Notice that I did not feel optimistic about finding a parking space, yet I chose to persist regardless of my pessimism. I acknowledged my feelings, readjusted my thoughts to allow for the parking space to appear, and there it was.

- Janet noticed that her husband had fallen into a pattern of belittling her. She complained to her spouse that he never gave her a compliment. He looked at her in disbelief and said, "I just gave you a compliment not 2 minutes ago." He recounted what he said and Janet realized she is in a reactive state with her husband, not able to be in the moment. Her expectations were screening out what was happening right in front of her.

- Remember the story of Robert Greenburg from Week Two? Robert is the CEO who had a brilliant idea for a bionic eye. After many disappointments, he made a critical shift in his staffing. He hired only those people who wholeheartedly believed that the project was possible. The young engineers he hired did not have the scotoma that the more senior engineers had. The project was successful because these young engineers were unschooled in the traditional thinking of what was possible.

- Back in Week One, I wrote about how I made the fundamental choice to be a healing force on the planet and this is what led me to shamanism. What I did not mention was the incredible resistance I had to believing shamanic methods were valid and Helping Spirits were real. After my first exposure to shamanism, I literally spent years denying that the Spirits I had interacted with during my journeys were actual beings. I was sure I had made them up in my imagination. Because of my cultural and religious training, I had no context to put them into. I had a big fat scotoma stopping me from fully entering into the wondrous magical world of shamanic healing. It was only when I began to receive accurate information from these Spirits that was not obtainable by ordinary means that I recognized my scotoma and was able to make the choice to move past it, beyond my childhood and societal conditioning. Once recognized, the scotoma did not magically disappear. This scotoma was an ingrained pattern and I had to surround myself with people I trusted who would continually challenge and support me to move past this particular scotoma.

How has your sense of what is real been influenced by what you are taught to believe is possible?

_____

_____

_____

_____

_____

What dreams have you curtailed because you could not see beyond your perceptions?

_____

_____

_____

_____

_____

How have you allowed fear to limit your ability to perceive clearly?

_____

_____

_____

_____

_____

_____

_____

_____

And the best question yet: How can you see past your scotomas and move into the expansive state of drawing to you what is possible?

_____

_____

_____

_____

_____

_____

_____

_____

Here are some ideas from the worlds of ordinary reality and non-ordinary reality to get you started:

- ❖ Change your expectancy outlook. Act as if everything is available to you now. Focus on your vision, the observable present and notice the excited expectancy. Act as if the answer is coming—because it is—and you will start noticing ways to attain your vision. Allow the possibilities in. You can start small: remember I started with a yellow-headed blackbird.

- ❖ Rub elbows with people who inspire you and do things differently. Look for role models and thought leaders. Look for those people who break through barriers you think are impossible for you to break through. Maybe it is someone who has figured out how to support himself without a regular job or someone who travels to those places you would love to go. Or someone who has an attitude that helps her to create outrageously great results. Although you may feel intimidated to ask these people for advice and mentoring, these are the very people that can help you to get over your limitations about how to see the world. They are doing it. Likely, they remember when they were struggling to move past their own limitations and will be happy to talk with you. And ask yourself the question: "How can I do that?" Better yet, "How can I do what they did, only better, bigger, with my unique stamp upon it?" How do you find these people? Affirm to yourself that they are right where you are: examining fruit at the grocery store, lurking at the buffet table at the party, and picking their mail up at the post office. If you cannot find these people, you can listen to them online at Ted.com.

- ❖ Ask your Helping Spirits. You have been working with these spirits now for several weeks. They are excellent candidates for advice as they have no preconceptions about what is possible. And also inquire if there is a new Helping Spirit for you to meet that would specifically help you to overcome your scotomas. Ask for assistance in letting go of the fear that blocks your ability to co-create.

If you are always expecting that there are not going to be parking places by the front entrance or that the person you need to reach is unavailable, then you simply are not going to perceive them *even if they are right in front of you*. Really wonderful things could be happening to you as a result of your manifestation work, but unless you recognize the scotomas that prevent you from perceiving what is happening, you will not *see* your results. So learn to recognize your scotomas and notice what possibilities are there for you so you can move forward with your goals.

What I am about to tell you is a very common way that people sabotage themselves in the Co-Creation Process. You've all witnessed it and you've all done it. It's the one thing that will trip you up more than anything else. When you do this, spontaneity goes out the window and stagnation comes in. It prevents leaping forward; it prevents changing the old pattern to allow fresh insights. Can you guess what it is?

It is over preparing.

Solutions for Over Preparing

You have a goal. You are excited. After the initial excitement, you begin to think that before you can move forward with the goal, you really need to do some more preparation.

You have created a checklist of items that must be done before you can get to your goal. After all, you do not want to (pick one): fail, look stupid, not know all the answers, have the wrong materials, show up at the wrong time in the wrong place wearing the wrong clothes. So you begin to prepare. And gosh darn it, all of a sudden there are a million things you need to prepare for, just in case.

And then there are the things you must do with the rest of your life before you can jump into this new thing. You decide to tie up all loose ends so you will not be distracted once you jump into your new goal. Some checklists often include things like: check e-mail, design business cards, type up all your notes and put them in a notebook, clear off the desk, take out the trash, call up that friend you have forgotten to call . . .

Guess what? You have just sabotaged yourself by diverting and diffusing your momentum. You are responding to distress. The result is you spend all your time preparing and never do get into action. Or you get started so slowly, you have lost valuable time. Or after your initial enthusiasm has worn off, you convince yourself the effort to start is just not worth it. It's too late, it's over and the opportunity is no longer there, or so you believe.

If this describes you, take heart. It really describes almost everyone at some point. Who hasn't frozen like a rabbit when we are faced with a new challenge or new information we need to digest and move on with in a hurry? Many find it easier to get sidetracked by doing familiar tasks when confronted with starting something new and different.

The good news is you *can* learn how to process and move quickly. All it takes is your willingness. Study the masters. Find someone you admire, either in your personal life or someone you can at least observe. And watch how they do it. What questions do they ask? Do they sometimes fall short of their vision? Do they have a Plan B, just in case? Do they look at failures as an opportunity to learn and move on? Successful people often have the philosophy that failure is good because failure teaches them they are stretching their limits. And it shows that they are not over preparing. They want to be on the edge, doing as much as possible with a good rate (not a perfect rate) of success. You may also notice that successful people do not judge themselves. They make an assessment about their results, modify if necessary and then they move on. They don't look back. Fast growing, nimble companies that must stay responsive to demand echo this philosophy as stated by Salesforce.com's visionary founder, chairman and CEO, Marc Benioff, "It's better to have a culture that encourages the acknowledgment of mistakes and gives everyone the opportunity to learn from them. Don't get me wrong—everyone on our team knows making the same mistakes is unacceptable, but they also know that a person making no mistakes is likely doing so because they are taking no risks and likely accomplishing nothing toward the firm's innovation."[21]

Also consider adding structure to your day that includes your new goals. I find it helpful to set aside a definite time when I will be working on my creative projects. When the time arrives, I shut down my distractions and keep a watch close by. I get up every 20 minutes and stretch. I do not answer the phone. For many months I resisted this structure, believing my creative projects would develop organically. What I finally understood is I needed to provide dedicated space in my life for new developments to occur. Yes, the Universe does command the big picture but I have my part to play. My part is paying attention, providing space for creative ah-ha's to happen, and faithfully persisting despite opposition—mostly my own.

Here is a way I found to counteract the urge to over prepare: taking a leap.

When I first began offering shamanic trainings, I found that my Helping Spirits were very inspirational. They would gift me with an idea for a workshop. My next step was to create a flier and send it out immediately, even though I had only the barest idea of the content and the title. Within a few days I would have enough sign-ups to make the workshop a "go." I would then devote myself to developing the details of the presentations. I discovered over time that this was the very best way for me to create workshops. The Spirits could sense when a topic was important and timely. My only assignment was to go with the momentum and not slow down the process.

I had to step out of the way and trust that everything was unfolding perfectly. And once the workshop was a "go," I had to trust the Spirits to come through and provide me with the rest of the content.

In shamanic literature, we talk about how shamans are the hollow bones for the transmission of healing powers to their clients and community. This means that first the shaman has to get their ego out of the way.

Creativity is no different. All those thoughts about how stupid you look, how half-baked this idea is or how unprepared you are have to be released in the interest of serving the idea whose time has come.

> Your vision or goal is not here to serve you. You are in service to your vision. You have to yield your ego to allow the grace of a transpersonal power to come in.

The hollow bone concept has helped me a great deal. When I first began to work on this book, I became overwhelmed with inner objections and lack of confidence. I would fritter away my writing time with minutiae, succumbing to my anxiety about my abilities as a writer. It was only when my students told me how they had been helped by this material that I realized this book was not about me being a writer. This book had many more people to help and if I was not going get my ego out of the way and allow the material to come through me, the Spirits would find someone who would. I would never be prepared enough. I had to trust the Divine muses to evolve the book through me as I willingly opened to their inspirations.

Consider your visions and goals. Are they really about you? Or is there a greater purpose to them? How do your goals relate to your family, community, planet, and descendants? Imagine being at the end of your life and looking over the years, what legacy would you want to leave for future generations, for your children and their children?

While you are studying this new area, continue to work with the three point process of:

     ◇   visualizing the goal,

     ◇   telling the truth about the observable present, and

     ◇   noticing the creative tension and feeling the excited expectancy.

Action Steps: Week Seven

- Continue with the Audio Program, choosing the Week Seven tracks, "Week Seven AM" and "Week Seven PM."

- Ask your Helping Spirits for help with expanding your view of reality especially as it relates to your stretch goal.

- Continue reading your Personal Statement twice per day with passion.

- Journal work: document your progress toward your stretch goal.

- Journal work: record what steps you are taking to move quickly towards your stretch goal.

- Journal: review past "mistakes" (can be from any period of your life). What have you learned? What new pathways opened as a result of your "mistakes?"

- Journal work: record scotomas as you remember them from your past and as they appear now. Ask other people what scotomas they have experienced.

- Ask yourself: "What one small thing in my life would I like to change but do not believe I can?" Ask your Helping Spirits for assistance with this.

- Read your list of "Things I Choose to Manifest" each day.

WEEK EIGHT

Acknowledgement and Blessings

CONGRATULATIONS ON MAKING it to Week Eight! Your brain has now made new connections that are serving you as you become the Predominant Creative Force in your life. You have new ways of thinking and being. You have learned to open up to the possibilities of the Universe and to create excited expectancy propelling you ever faster towards your dreams.

Before we continue, let's take a moment to acknowledge how far you have come in your Co-Creation journey. You've learned how to choose happiness and how happiness supports you when you enter the Universal flow of Co-Creation. You learned how to vision, acknowledge the creative tension and use that excited expectancy to propel you towards your vision. You developed a long term vision for yourself when you tackled the Personal Statement and by now, you are feeling an inner alignment with your Personal Statement. You learned that the Universe works in synchronistic ways and you also learned ways to recognize scotomas in your life. You have examined the boundaries in your life and how healthy boundaries contribute to your effectiveness as a creative person. You have recognized the role of spirituality in Co-Creation and how to call on the great powers for assistance and guidance. You have learned to move forward even when you feel vulnerable and not quite ready. You have learned about the power of persistence. And most important, you have been an active participant in realigning your brain chemistry to recognize yourself as a co-creative, powerful agent of change in your Universe.

If you continue to utilize these methods, you will become a master manifestor, able to create change for yourself and impact the world in a positive way.

Now I will introduce you to two more powerful tools for you to use: acknowledgement and blessings.

The Power of Acknowledgement

> *If you obsess over whether you are making the right decision, you are basically assuming that the Universe will reward you for one thing and punish you for another.*
>
> *The Universe has no fixed agenda. Once you make any decision, it works around that decision. There is no right or wrong, only a series of possibilities that shift with each thought, feeling, and action that you experience.*
>
> —Deepak Chopra

As you acknowledge your progress notice how easily your subconscious supports you. Acknowledgment is a necessary component for successful manifestation. Acknowledgement provides fertile ground to ensure future creative endeavors will take hold. If you acknowledge even tiny bits of progress, then your subconscious gets the message that you are moving towards your goals and becomes an eager supporter of those aspirations you hold most dear.

Those who are perfectionists or those who are always trying harder may be reluctant to give themselves permission to recognize and celebrate small successes. They may feel they can only acknowledge their progress when exactly what they wanted to manifest is achieved.

Watch out for that! The journey to your goal is comprised of many small successes. Acknowledge each small success and your subconscious will get the message. Find a physical movement to validate each small success. Try a high five, a victory dance, or reaching your arms up to the sky and shouting "YES!"

If you focus on qualities you want to develop, such as compassion, patience, or gratitude, it can be difficult to quantify when you have reached your goal.

Let's take a look at Anna, who intends to develop the quality of patience. She carefully monitors herself throughout the day and notes that she is sometimes impatient with her elderly mother. Anna feels badly about this and concludes she has made no progress towards her goal. She concludes she is an impatient person.

At the end of the day, Anna feels she has nothing to celebrate because she experienced impatience with her mother. I asked Anna if there were other times during the day when she had been patient. She said that yes there were but she had not counted those.

Anna felt she had to be perfect to reach her goal. In fact, Anna had been patient in the majority of her interactions but had not acknowledged herself because there was one interaction where she failed to be patient.

The solution is to acknowledge and celebrate progress, even small progress. As you acknowledge progress, you train your subconscious to recognize movement. When you consistently acknowledge that you are making advances with your goals, you find your intentions are leading you forward, and the subconscious accepts that you are the Predominant Creative Force in your life. You affirm to the subconscious that small steps are good and micro successes are a reason to celebrate. The subconscious then helps you to continue to create, leading you to even greater successes. The subconscious jumps on the momentum bandwagon. This is positive upward spiral made up of small positive steps. Micro successes lead to bigger successes.

I asked Anna to now track each interaction and rate herself on the quality of patience. She was surprised to notice that she has a great track record with everyone else except her mother and could readily acknowledge herself as being a patient person. She still has the intention of being even more patient with her mother, but now she has a positive foundation to build on. Now her subconscious is learning that she is already a patient person and Anna is expecting to find some creative ways to be patient in her next interaction with her mother.

An important point here is that Anna did not give up on her intention of becoming a patient person. She noted where she failed to meet her criteria of patience and then began to track her results. She found herself to generally be a patient person and gave her subconscious factual information so that in the future her subconscious could be more creative in coming up with ways to be patient with her mother.

Failure is a very judgmental word. It implies that your result is an all or nothing. But failure is rarely 100%. Count up the successes and acknowledge those. If necessary, reformulate the intention more precisely and start moving again towards your desired goal. We are always learning, taking in new information, assessing, juggling possibilities and making adjustments.

Disappointment is a fact of life. I will not lead you on a trip through a landscape where only good things happen and you never have to face bad news. While we all experience some disappointment in our lives, those who follow the Co-Creation Process know that failure is simply a label we attach to our experience in the observable present. Our perception of the observable present can change in a heartbeat. And we can be the one that willingly decides our perception needs to change. And we can change it.

Think back to a time when you were sure you would be hearing some bad news. Did you feel angry, depressed, sad? When the real news came in and it was good news, did you notice how quickly your emotions changed and how suddenly you were on top of the world? Many people can relate to this in the area of job searches, college applications, relationships, and health test results.

Your emotions, so fickle, are only powerful if you give them power. You have a choice to inform yourself that while you may hear disappointing news, you do have a choice about how you respond. While others may be forthcoming with their opinion about what results you may expect, remember it is their opinion—but it is your life. Successful people all moved forward despite what other people thought.

Great manifestors can recount many examples of how they were often disappointed as they moved towards their goals. They chose to learn from disappointment. When they ran into dead ends, they made adjustments and continued on towards their goals. They accepted disappointment as part of the process, not the end result. They chose to persist. They persisted by telling the truth about their observable present by acting as their own Fair Witness, and then focusing on the vision. They noticed the creative tension and felt the excitement of their vision. And once again, they began to move forward toward their goal.

Here is one of my favorite stories about the observable present and the foolishness of labeling events good or bad.

Good Luck Bad Luck!

There is a Chinese story of a farmer who used an old horse to till his fields. One day, the horse escaped into the hills and when the farmer's neighbors sympathized with the old man over his bad luck, the farmer replied, "Bad luck? Good luck? Who knows?" A week later, the horse returned with a herd of horses from the hills and this time the neighbors congratulated the farmer on his good luck. His reply was, "Good luck? Bad luck? Who knows?"

Then, when the farmer's son was attempting to tame one of the wild horses, he fell off its back and broke his leg. Everyone thought this very bad luck. Not the farmer, whose only reaction was, "Bad luck? Good luck? Who knows?"

Some weeks later, the army marched into the village and conscripted every able-bodied youth they found there. When they saw the farmer's son with his broken leg, they let him off. Now was that good luck or bad luck?

Who knows?

—Author Unknown

What I love about this story is that it helps me realize that there is no such thing as luck. There are turns of events. What we do with those events with our conscious intention is what makes all the difference.

The Power of Blessings

THE SECOND AREA of acknowledgement is to recognize others. Some of the reasons to do this are to keep the creativity flowing, to facilitate success by encouragement, and to engender a positive environment so everyone is uplifted and more open to seeing how they can move forward and receive.

You may have heard of this experiment in college psychology classes. The students are given four paper cups with soil and one bean seed is planted in each cup. Each cup receives the same amount of water and sunshine. Their daily assignment is this:

The students are to stand in front of their first cup and think good thoughts.

For the second cup they are to say: "I want you to be at least eighteen inches tall, have at least fifteen branches and produce at least thirty beans before you are done."

For the third cup, they are to insult the bean sprout with words such as "You are stupid. You are worthless."

For the fourth cup, they are to simply say, "God bless this bean sprout."

At the end of the semester, they analyzed their results. Amazingly the bean sprout that did the poorest was in the second cup, the cup of high expectations. Expecting specific outcomes produced the poorest result. So we see again how important it is to not attach to the HOW's. The insulted cup and the good thoughts cups did about the same. And the fourth simply blessed sprout was about three times bigger than any of the others.

I decided to run this experiment myself. My sample size was eight for each condition. Each day I spent about ten seconds in front of each group of beans thinking the required thoughts. At the end of the twenty-one day experiment, the bean sprouts in the worthless category were stunted. Some of the sprouts were truncated and withered even though I had physically protected them from any tampering. The blessed and good thoughts sprouts did very well; all these sprouts grew robustly and very tall.

From this experiment we can deduce that a blessing of goodwill not attached to specific outcomes produces the best results. Blessings are powerful!

"Have a great day!" How many times have you heard this? This is a common way for store clerks and acquaintances to end a conversation. Did you know this is also a blessing? Blessings are a powerful way to set intention for another by offering those qualities that everyone wants. Who would say no to "a great day?"

I grew up as most of us did receiving blessings from the church pastor or priest or from my elder relatives. We spoke our blessings awkwardly around the Thanksgiving table. We blessed the food and gave thanks for our good fortune, our family, and our lives. This way of experiencing blessings is a form of prayer.

I first encountered the idea that blessings could reside outside a religious context from Martín Prechtel. Martín is a brilliant writer and teacher who assists his students in reconnecting to the sacredness in nature and everyday life.

One day Martín sent us out to ask for a blessing from a homeless person. He told us that to ask for a blessing from such a person did them a great honor for it acknowledged the power they retain despite their circumstances. And that kind of power is the strongest. It is the power to persist and to be ourselves in the face of adversity.

He taught us to see these people as complete and holy. He also taught us to write "love letters to the Goddess," to that which is sacred in our lives, and to give these love letters away freely to strangers as a blessing. As I gave these letters away to strangers I fumbled for the right words to tell them what this little folded up piece of paper was, and then I saw their faces transformed with joy and delight. No one ever refused my poem gifts.

In his book, *Blessing, The Art and The Practice,*[22] author David Spangler defines a blessing as a way of affirming our connection to one another:

> *A blessing is much more than just an act. It is an affirmation of our interconnectedness. It is the creation of an opportunity for the power of that connectedness to pour through into our lives and the lives of others. So in practicing the art of blessing, we are really practicing being connected. We are practicing how to discover and express those parts of ourselves that innately understand that connectedness and the wholeness that emerges from it.*

Asking someone for a blessing is a way to affirm our connectedness and also to affirm their power. In asking for a blessing, we put ourselves in a vulnerable position. We are asking for their goodwill, a type of help. There is no vision without vulnerability.

And here lies the lesson: if we hoard power for ourselves by being self serving, we won't be given much. We will be out of the flow and disconnected. If we use our power to heal, enlighten, inspire, and to honor, we're giving back and completing the circle. And to acknowledge the holiness in each of us is a concrete way for us to acknowledge the holiness in everything. And so we return to the circle and our understanding that energy and power flow in a circle: as we give blessings out, more and more come back. The more you open up, the more comes through, the more you let go, the more it comes back. And so we come full circle to the Universal laws:

As above, so below. As within, so without.

Blessings can be your everyday vehicle for opening up to more of the Universal flow, opening up and sharing more power, love, joy, and happiness with those around you—even those you do not know.

Giving a blessing is like giving a gift. We cannot be attached to how it is received or how it is used. While we may want to bless a person to help them with their failed relationship, the energy we are sending cannot be directed so specifically. It is best to simply beam the light of the blessing energy to the person and allow them to absorb this wherever it is needed. How do you construct a blessing? I think the best way is to simply say, "Bless you!"

My favorite way to give a blessing is to request my Helping Spirits to join me and send the Universal powers of love and healing through me to the person as a blessing.

Here are some blessings that I am especially fond of. These are particularly good for gatherings or ceremonies. May you draw your own favorites to you and repeat them always that you may be reminded of the power of the circle of life.

This first one is a song that we sing in shamanic circles:

May you walk in beauty in a sacred way

May you walk in beauty each and every day

May the beauty of the fire lift your spirit higher

May the beauty of the rain take away your pain

May the beauty of the earth fill your heart with mirth

May the beauty of the sky teach your mind to fly.

A Blessing of Solitude

May you recognize in your life, the presence, power and light of your soul.

May you realize that you are never alone,

That your soul in its brightness and belonging

connects you intimately with the rhythm of the universe.

May you have respect for your own individuality and difference.

May you realize that the shape of your soul is unique,

that you have a special destiny here,

That behind the facade of your life

there is something beautiful, good, and eternal happening.

May you learn to see yourself with the same delight, pride,

and expectation with which God sees you in every moment.[23]

—John O'Donohue

An Old Irish Blessing

May the road rise up to meet you.

May the wind always be at your back.

May the sun shine warm upon your face,

and rains fall soft upon your fields.

And until we meet again,

May God hold you in the palm of His hand.

What if you don't feel like giving a blessing? What if everything is going wrong and you don't believe in the blessing? The trick is to give the blessing anyway. Because in the great circle of energetic flow, you can give a blessing when you feel crappy. Giving the blessing will help the other person feel blessed. *And* it will also help you to feel blessed. And you will feel better. Sometimes acting the part and putting forth the effort is all it takes to make a shift. That's how the flow of energy in this great circle of life works.

Moving Forward

ONCE YOU HAVE completed this eight week journey, you may feel the urge to drop the process as a reward for pursuing it to the end. Remember that persistence and a willingness to be an active Co-Creator are the key attributes of successful manifestors. Keep the process going and watch your life light up! All successful manifestors continue to do those things that help them to keep co-creating at a rapid rate. If you own a high performance car, you give it a high octane gasoline since this is what it needs for optimal performance. The same goes for you as a high performance creator. You need to continue to nurture your growth and expand your ability to create. While eight weeks has given you a firm foundation on which to grow, there is still much growing to do. Continue to look for materials that will stimulate this growth. Keep up with the Audio Program, repeating those segments you find most helpful. Make your own audio files if you feel inspired to create ones especially suited for you. Continue to visit your Spirit Helpers with the drumming tracks and take them your questions. Listen to their answers. Continue to work with new stretch goals and visions. Over time you will find these come to fruition quicker and with much less effort than before. Continue to refine your Personal Statement because you are changing and the statement is a living breathing reflection of your future new self.

Audio Program

NOW YOU ARE about to take a major leap forward with your Co-Creation skills. This week the audio track selections are no longer guided visualizations. This week you will be free to undertake your audio time as unguided shamanic journeys. There are two drumming tracks. One is ten minutes long with a return and the other is twenty minutes long with a return. You have heard the drumming in the background of each audio track to date. Your assignment is to journey with these drumming tracks to either the lower or upper worlds and ask your Helping Spirits for guidance. Your specific questions are below in the homework. But you can also expand on those questions and utilize your shamanic journey time for other matters. Remember to always set a clear intention and have specific questions to take to your Spirit Helpers.

To re-cap, you will start out in a place in nature that you truly love. You will listen to the drumming for a few minutes until you are ready to give your full attention to the journey. Then you will open all of your senses including smell, sight, hearing, feeling, taste and knowing/intuiting. Once you are as present as you can be, look for a way to go down to the Lower World or a way to go up to the Upper World. Go in whichever direction you feel called. Once there, find your Helping Spirits and ask them for their advice.

You can journey for ten minutes or twenty minutes. If the return beat comes before you are ready to end the journey, you can simply start the drumming track over again. When you do hear the return, carefully and conscientiously retrace your steps back to your place in nature. Open your eyes and write down your answers. If you would like to pursue further training in the shamanic journey, there are several organizations that offer shamanic training and helpful books in the Resource section at the back.

Action Steps: Week Eight

- Continue with the Audio Program this time using the tracks labeled: 10-Minute Drumming with Return and 20-minute Drumming with Return. Listen to Week Eight Intro your first time through to receive your instructions.

- Each day choose one of the following questions to ask your Helping Spirits:

  - ◇ How can I be of service to those around me and to this planet?
  - ◇ How can I best acknowledge and celebrate my growth over these eight weeks?
  - ◇ How can I acknowledge and bless those around me?
  - ◇ What are my next steps in co-creating?

- Continue reading your Personal Statement twice per day with passion.

- About every 6 months, update your Personal Statement, more often if needed, to stay relevant.

- Document your progress towards your stretch goal.

- Each day this week list 10 small successes.

- Find concrete ways to celebrate your successes.

- Practice the art of blessing yourself, your friends, and strangers. Bless once per day . . . even your cat or dog! Especially bless when you feel down. Notice how you feel afterwards.

- Read your list of "Things I Choose to Manifest" each day.

- Celebrate your successful completion of this training!

Resources for Further Shamanic Training

To find a shamanic teacher or practitioner in your area:

Foundation for Shamanic Studies at Shamanism.org
Shamanicteachers.com
Society for Shamanic Practitioners at Shamansociety.org

Books:

Shamanic Journeying: a Beginner's Guide by Sandra Ingerman
The Way of the Shaman by Michael Harner

Bibliography

Arrien, Angeles. *The Four -Fold Way: Walking the Paths of the Warrior, Teacher, Healer, and Visionary.* San Francisco: HarperCollins, 1993.

Castaneda, Carlos. *Journey to Ixtlan.* New York: Simon & Shuster, 1975.

Chödrön, Pema. *Start Where You Are: A Guide to Compassionate Living.* Boston: Shambala, 2004.

Chard, Philip Sutton. *The Healing Earth: Nature's Medicine for the Troubled Soul.* Minnetonka: Northwood Press, 1994.

Dooley, Mike. *Infinite Possibilities: The Art of Living Your Dreams.* New York: Atria Books, 2009. www.tut.com

Foxwood, Orion. *Tree of Enchantment: Ancient Wisdom and Magic Practices of the Faery Tradition.* San Francisco: Weiser Books, 2008.

Fritz, Robert. *The Path of Least Resistance: Principles for Creating What You Want to Create.* DMA, 1984 edition.

Grout, Pam. *E-squared: Nine Do-It-Yourself Experiments that Prove Your Thoughts Create Your Reality.* New York: Hay House, 2013.

Heinlein, Robert A. *Stranger in a Strange Land.* New York: G.P. Putnam's Sons, 1961.

Hermes Trimegistus. *The Emerald Tablet of Hermes & The Kybalion.* Create Space Independent Publishing Platform, 2008.

Ingerman, Sandra. *Soul Retrieval: Mending the Fragmented Self.* San Francisco: Harper, 1991.

Laszlo, Ervin. *The New Science and Spirituality Reader.* Rochester, VT: Inner Traditions, 2012.

_____. *You Can Change the World.* New York: Select Books, 2003.

McGonigal, Kelly, PhD. "The Neuroscience of Change." From an interview with Tami Simon, Sounds True, April 19, 2012.

Mills, Billy. *Wokini: Your Personal Journey to Happiness and Self-Understanding.* Feather Publishing, 1990 edition.

Neville. *The Neville Reader.* Camarillo, CA:DeVorss & Co, 2005.

Peterson, Roger Tory, *A Field Guide to Eastern Birds*, 4th Ed. Boston: Houghton Mifflin, 1980.

Spangler, David. *Blessing: The Art and the Practice.* New York: Riverhead

Trade, 2002.

_____. *Everyday Miracles: The Inner Art of Manifestation.* Everett, WA: Lorian Press, 2008.

_____*Subtle Worlds: An Explorer's Field Notes.* Everett, WA: Lorian Press, 2010.

Notes

1   Kelly McGonigal, Ph.D. "The Neuroscience of Change." Audio interview. Sounds True. April 19, 2012.

2   Robert Fritz. *The Path of Least Resistance,* 1985. The phrase "Predominant Creative Force" was first coined by Robert Fritz in this groundbreaking book.

3   Marci Shimoff & Carol Kline. *Happy for No Reason: 7 Steps to Being Happy from the Inside Out, 2009.*

4   *The Emerald Tablet,* also known as Smaragdine Table, Tabula Smaragdina, or The Secret of Hermes, is a text purporting to reveal the secret of the primordial substance and its transmutations. It claims to be the work of Hermes Trismegistus ("Hermes the Thrice-Greatest"), a legendary Hellenistic combination of the Greek god Hermes and the Egyptian god Thoth.

5   "Thoughts become things, thus the very act of thinking something endows thoughts with life. All is flux, nothing stays still." Heraclitus.

6   Shawn Achor. *The Happiness Advantage: The Seven Principles of Positive Psychology that Fuel Success and Performance at Work.* Crown Business, 2010.

7   The Happiness Institute. This discussion can be found at their website www.happinessresearchinstitute.com/rich-or-happy/4578771603. Through a number of surveys, the economist Richard Easterlin has investigated the paradox between countries' growth in economy and level of happiness. For example, the American economy has tripled per inhabitant since 1960, while the average level of happiness is unaltered.

8   Billy Mills. *Wokini: Your Personal Journey to Happiness and Self-Understanding,* 1990. Feather Publishing Company. P43.

9. Watkins, Philip C., et al. *"Gratitude and happiness: Development of a measure of gratitude, and relationships with subjective well-being." Social Behavior and Personality: an international journal* 32.5 (2003): 431-451.

10 Michael Benoist. *"Climber Who Cuts Off Hand Looks Back."* National Geographic Adventure, August 30, 2004.

11 Brandelyn Rose is the creator of a band steadily gaining in popularity

and playing to crowds of over 3000. They have cut three CD's and are based in Eugene Oregon. Featured as part of Relix magazine's "Bands on the Rise" and voted "Best New Act" by the WOW hall in Eugene OR. Formed in 2011 after a "chance" encounter at the Oregon Country Fair, singer/songwriter Brandelyn Rose and 16-year old guitar prodigy Felix Blades sparked a unique and collaborative friendship that has attracted other talented artists.

12 Melinda Maxfield, Ph.D. Abstract: *"Effects of Rhythmic Drumming on EEG and Subjective Experience,"* Institute of Transpersonal Psychology, 1990, 167 pages; DP14292

13 Ronald D. White. *"Bionic Eye Maker has Vision of the Future."* Los Angeles Times, April 27, 2013.

14 This is an adaptation of a ceremony taught to me by Sandra Ingerman.

15 Napoleon Hill. *Think and Grow Rich.* Best Success Books, 2008. This is a modified format based on Hill's work.

16 Rhonda Whetham's website is http://aromajourney.com

17 Rock grinding is an ancient method of shamanic initiation practiced by Greenland Eskimos as late as the 19th century. The initiate goes out to the wilderness alone and finds two rocks to rub together with a circular motion for hours producing a hypnotic state. The compassionate beings often come forth taking the initiate on journeys into non-ordinary reality where he or she may meet Helping Spirits in the form of wild animals or spiritual teachers and may be given guidance and healing powers.

18 Marc Nepo. *The Book of Awakening: Having the Life You Want by Being Present to the Life You Have,* Conari Press, 2000.

19 Stephanie Winston. *The Organized Executive,* Business Plus, 2001.

20 Ernest Laszlo. *Science and the Akashic Field: An Integral Theory of Everything,* Inner Traditions, 2004.

21 Marc Benioff. *Behind the Cloud.* Hoboken, NJ: Jossey-Bass, 2009.

22 David Spangler. *Blessing, The Art and The Practice.* Riverhead Books New York. 2002.

23 John O'Donohue. *Anam Cara, A Book of Celtic Wisdom.* Harper Collins. 1998.

Acknowledgements

I BEGIN WITH gratitude for my life and all of life, the blessing I experience each moment with each breath.

I thank my husband, Reid Hart, for his unwavering support, encouragement and love and for believing in me always.

I thank Earl Strumpell, my editor, for helping me to find my voice with his constant encouragement, curiosity and friendship. I thank Linda Leanne of Inner Rhythms who skillfully and sensitively guided me through the Audio Program recording. Catherine Van Wetter I thank for her wordsmithing of the Audio Program.

I thank Patricia Marshall of Luminare Press for skillfully bringing my book from manuscript to final product.

I thank Shelley Masters of Shelley Masters Studio, inspired artist and clear channel to the Spirits, for her painting gracing the cover of this book.

I acknowledge the brilliant work of Robert Fritz, author of The Path of Least Resistance. His concepts launched me on a thirty year journey to understand creativity. Among all the writers on creativity, he is the clearest and most helpful conceptually. His terms 'fundamental choice', 'primary choice', 'secondary choice' and 'Predominant Creative Force', among others, are used throughout this book.

I thank my shamanic community and Hearth of the Dancing Drum healing and drumming circles for their love and support and always showing up these past twenty two years.

I thank my students and colleagues who have participated in the birthing of this book, who adventurously followed the Co-Creation Handbook from start to finish and showed me it was indeed work that needed to be shared.

CPSIA information can be obtained
at www.ICGtesting.com
Printed in the USA
FSHW020935101118
53704FS

9 781937 303396